D1356778

Ecology and Land Use in Upland Scotland

Ecology and Land Use in Upland Scotland by D.N.McVean and J.D.Lockie. Edinburgh, at the University Press

© Copyright 1969
D.N. McVean and J.D. Lockie
EDINBURGH UNIVERSITY PRESS
22 George Square, Edinburgh
North America
Aldine Publishing Company
529 South Wabash Avenue, Chicago
85224 160 7
Library of Congress
Catalog Card Number 70-92288
Printed in Great Britain by
Robert Cunningham & Sons Ltd, Alva

Contents

Preface *p. ix*

Introduction *p. 1*

1. The Upland Environment *p. 6*

2. Geological and Accelerated Erosion of Soil and Peat *p. 24*

3. Hill Farming *p. 36*

4. Forestry *p. 55*

5. Sport and the Game Animals *p. 66*

6. Habitat and Wildlife Conservation *p. 85*

7. Tourism *p. 98*

8. Multi-Purpose Land Use and the Future *p. 103*

List of Plant and Animal Names *p. 115*

Glossary *p. 118*

Bibliography *p. 121*

Index *p. 128*

List of Illustrations

Figures

1. Areas with and without potential water deficit in Scotland *p. 15*
2. Vegetation map of the west Cairngorms *p. 112*
3. Land capability map of the west Cairngorms *p. 113*

Plates (at end)

1. Dense native Scots pine forest
2. Typical sheep-grazed west Highland birch wood
3. Ungrazed birch–rowan wood
4. Sheep-grazed ash wood on limestone pavement near Tornapress, Ross-shire
5. Typical heather-dominated hillside in the central Highlands, showing erosion
6. Sheet erosion of shallow peat at 1,000 feet on quartzite
7. Scree formation, destruction of juniper and breaking of *Agrostis–Festuca* turf by grazing and burning
8. Active gullying in Glen Tilt by grazing and trampling
9. End point of deep peat erosion
10. Gully erosion in the south-west Highlands as a result of grazing and burning
11. Sheet erosion and gullying contrasted with intact afforested land
12. Sheet erosion and bunkers on land previously forested and now heavily grazed
13. Wind erosion of machair at Opinan, Ross-shire
14. Erosion caused by tourism in the north Cairngorms
15. Bracken spreading into heather after a burn
16. Red deer stag on low ground in winter
17. Good wintering ground in the Cairngorms
18. Birch thicket, naturally regenerated and under heavy browsing pressure

Preface

So many branches of the earth and life sciences meet and anastomose in the fields of ecology and land use that two individuals between them cannot hope to be conversant with all matters, nor avoid giving some offence to specialists when venturing to write about the interaction of two subjects which are themselves interdisciplinary. Ecology itself is not so much a discrete field of knowledge as an attitude of mind in which to approach all biology; the ecological point of view can now be discerned, for example, in the literature of human sociology and pathology. Land use ecology, therefore, is simply the ecological approach to all forms of land use, although frequently excluding urban and other civil engineering development. Although *Man and Nature* by George Perkins Marsh, published in 1864, is generally considered to mark the commencement of the ecological viewpoint in land use and to represent the first plea for conservation, it is only twenty years since the first specific text on land use ecology appeared —Edward Graham's *Natural Principles of Land Use*.

Over the last few years there has been a quickening of interest in the ecology of land use in upland Britain, and our aim in writing this book has been to focus attention on certain aspects, relating particularly to Scotland, that have been neglected or have been presented somewhat out of perspective. The stimulus to do so, and the model to be followed have been given by Chapter 4, 'The Ecology of Land Use' in Fraser Darling's *West Highland Survey*, which presented for the first time the ecological setting of the whole 'Highland Problem'.

The factors at work in shaping the upland environment will be considered first, and this will be followed by a discussion of various ecological situations and problems divided for convenience into chapters on hill farming, forestry, nature conservation, and so on, although many of the topics would be appropriate under more than one heading. In a final chapter the prospects for greater diversity of land use in parts of the Scottish uplands will be considered and some suggestions made as to how this might be achieved. Much of the discussion is relevant to both the Highlands and Southern Uplands, but where remarks are applicable to a restricted area only this has been made clear.

Some previous knowledge of rocks, soils, plants, and animals on the part of the reader has been assumed, but some of the technical terms that could not be avoided are explained in a short glossary.

Post-graduate courses in conservation had been initiated by the

University College of London in 1960 and, following this lead, training in conservation and land use ecology is now available to students at Aberdeen, Edinburgh, and Bangor. The Department of Forestry and Natural Resources of Edinburgh University now offers degrees in Ecological Science with honours in Ecology, Forestry, Wildlife and Fisheries Management, and Resource Management. Aberdeen University initiated an M.SC. course in Ecology in 1965. It is to be hoped that the products of these schools will develop a reputation in the ecological approach to land management equal to that enjoyed by graduates in agriculture and forestry in their respective fields. In the relatively new field of nature conservation the land manager and the ecologist have each something to contribute to the common fund of knowledge and experience.

We should like to acknowledge the help given in discussion by members of the Nature Conservancy, Hill Farming Research Organization, Red Deer Commission, Forestry Commission, Macaulay Institute, and the Department of Forestry and Natural Resources in the University of Edinburgh. The interpretation of the data and the views expressed on man's relation with the Uplands of Scotland remain our responsibility.

We are indebted also to Dr R. M. Gorrie for permission to use plate 12, to F. Howie for plate 13, to David Stephen for plate 16, and to F. H. W. Green for figure 1.

Introduction

It is a tenet of the ecologists' approach to land use that renewable resources should be conserved and managed for a sustained yield rather than squandered for short-term advantage as has been done so often in the past; a simple enough concept, but often extraordinarily difficult to achieve in practice. The difference between the two systems is quite simply the difference between living on the interest from capital and living on the capital itself. Primitive peoples have managed to live on the interest from time to time, largely by leaving the existing ecosystem intact—and indeed becoming themselves part of it, thus living in harmony with their environment through thousands of years. On the other hand more advanced societies have sometimes been able to build up local soil fertility to a level that the interacting factors of climate, rocks, plants, and animals could not have attained unaided.

The climatic climax vegetation of an area can be an extremely productive system and is generally characterized by a wide variety of constituent species. Until recently ecologists speculated that it might, in fact, prove to be the most productive system possible at any place and that any interference with it would necessarily produce a reduction in overall productivity. Recent quantitative studies by McNaughton (1967) on the grasslands of California have supported an earlier finding by Margalef (1965) with marine plankton communities that high productivity tends to be associated with the dominance of a few species whereas stability of the community tends to be associated with species diversity. These conclusions, if found to be generally applicable, have obvious importance in land management. Productivity studies now being started under the auspices of the International Biological Programme may answer this question.

It has been known for some time, of course, that simple plant and animal communities, whether simple because of environmental severity or because interference by man has reduced them to a few dominant species, are more liable to wide and violent fluctuations in both plant and animal numbers. Put in another way, the simple communities are liable to plagues and sudden pest outbreaks. Variation in the population level of arctic hares and lemmings and in their predators, arctic foxes and snowy owls, are the classic examples of instability in a simple natural system. Vole plagues in a newly fenced forestry plantation illustrate the man-induced outbreak. All crops, agricultural and silvicultural, are inherently liable, through the simplicity of their structure, to sudden attacks by vast numbers of pests and by disease organisms. This has often to be accepted and it now looks as if secondary outbreaks produced by the chemical control of the primary pest may also have to be lived with for some time. The only alternative is the gradual introduction of biological control by highly selective organisms. In the management of natural or little-modified plant communities the fundamental remedy of increasing floristic diversity and structural complexity is theoretically possible and may be attempted.

Another important point which is often overlooked, and which has been emphasized particularly by Albrecht (1957), is that highly weathered, tropical soils and the calcium-deficient soils of high rainfall temperate regions alike are unsuitable for the production of protein crops, both plant and animal. The reasons for this are biochemical and concerned with the mineral requirements for protein synthesis, which are precise and found at their optimum only in limited areas of the world. Certain areas of unsuitable soil can be rendered suitable by application of the appropriate fertilizers, but the great majority of all soils in all climatic regions are capable of producing carbohydrate crops only, if they are to be conserved and remain in production. This includes irrigated desert soils.

One of the dangers inherent in protein cropping on intrinsically infertile soils by means of intensive fertilizer application is the tendency to neglect the organic matter in soil. When this falls to a low level, soil structure and stability are lost along with the micro-organisms that produce them, more intensive leaching and wholesale erosion occur, and the added fertilizers are then largely wasted.

There are several ways in which protein production can be forced from unsuitable soils apart from fertilizer application. Systematic moor burning, to be described in Chapter 3, is one of them. Protein production is here achieved only at the cost of considerable physical and chemical deterioration, culminating once again in soil erosion. The pattern of land use, therefore, should be based primarily upon the biochemical potentialities of the soil and climate.

The rate of circulation of mineral nutrients in the soil–vegetation complex is just as important as, and sometimes more important than, the total quantities present. The more rapid the circulation the more easily can the system be exploited and the more sensitive it is to misuse. It has been estimated by Albrecht (1957) that about three-quarters of present world crop production represents exploitation of the soil, that is, removal of fertility not made good in the form of organic or inorganic fertilizers. Some of this will be supplied by the natural processes of soil weathering, nitrogen fixation, and the addition of plant nutrients from the air, but a high proportion must represent loss of soil fertility capital.

Some principles of good land use, which are fundamentally ecological concepts, have long been accepted in agriculture. Thus, crop rotation and the incorporation of a leguminous break are accepted as beneficial and even essential, but the hill farmer who practises this system on his arable land fails to detect anything wrong with a wholly extractive regime on his continuously grazed hill ground.

For the last 200 years there has existed in British land use a startling dichotomy between the lowland and upland areas, between fertile farm land and land which is economically marginal or sub-marginal for any form of agriculture. On the one hand we have intensive husbandry, with soil fertility maintained or continually enhanced, on the other hand there is an almost entirely extractive pastoralism supported by direct and indirect cash subsidy. A well-farmed and thoroughly domesticated countryside and untouched, natural terrain with its vegetation and wildlife complexes intact can both be deeply satisfying. But an inherently infertile region devastated by deforestation and repeated burning, largely depopulated and then opened to heavy and uncontrolled sheep grazing is a distressing sight to anyone with some appreciation of ecological principles. This is the 'untouched wilderness' and 'rugged grandeur' that we are now being asked to 'sell' as a tourist attraction.

Within the last few decades re-appraisal of land use has begun in arid and semi-arid lands, perhaps because the impressive results of misuse have been most apparent in those regions where, as it happens, the control and redistribution of water supplies offers a relatively clear-cut solution to many of the problems. Cool, excessively humid lands with acid rocks and soils provide a different set of problems, and although such areas are less extensive they are worthy of some consideration also.

Let us take a look at some probable courses of events following occupation by man of a forested but infertile land in temperate or subtropical regions where the soil holds little of the available plant nutrients. The contrast that we would wish to make here is with a prairie environment or with a fertile temperate forest ecosystem, both of which hold the greater part of their mineral nutrient fund in the soil, where it can be exploited readily by cultivation and cropping. It is clear that the management of such contrasting biological systems must differ if they are to be conserved and provide a sustained yield.

The forest cover on the infertile site can be utilized by the controlled removal of timber and the harvesting of wild animals such as deer. Provided this exploitation is carefully regulated the ecosystem continues to yield a quantity of protein and wood products which can be surprisingly great in view of the poverty of the environment. Such an ecosystem keeps available mineral nutrients in circulation and the addition of nutrients from rock weathering and biological nitrogen fixation at a high level. The rate of addition of nutrients from the atmosphere too can be appreciable and remains constant whatever the state of the vegetation, but the retention of these nutrients depends on the activities of an intact soil and vegetation complex. At the same time more favoured pockets of soil, and there are usually some of these, can be intensively managed for crops and the grazing of domestic animals.

By present Western standards the living enjoyed by men in such an environment may be a poor one, and hence the total population small. Furthermore, the ecological balance is delicate and can easily be disturbed if, for example, the best trees are invariably extracted or if the forest is over-exploited for rough grazing to the exclusion of tree regeneration. Attempts to increase the rate of exploitation and utilize the resource capital directly by clear felling, extermination of wildlife, and stocking to the limit with domestic animals are disastrous. Deterioration may take either of two paths according to the local relationship between rainfall and evaporation.

Where the tendency is towards water deficits the weakened plant cover cannot resist the onset of soil erosion, water tables drop and aggravate both erosion and vegetation deterioration. The terrain then develops many of the characteristics of aridity, although the actual rainfall remains the same and quite capable of supporting high forest. Where the regional climatic tendency is towards water surpluses, on the other hand, the soil becomes wetter or completely waterlogged, nutrient circulation slows down and leaching becomes more active. As a result of this, bog plants increase and peat formation sets in and spreads. Mineral nutrients formerly in circulation become immobilized in the peat, and the moorland and bog vegetation which takes over the area possesses only a fraction of the productivity of the original forest. Where forest does manage to reoccupy part of the ground at a later date it differs from the original forest by forming even-aged patches dominated by one or two species only; these have difficulty in regeneration and their continued existence is precarious.

The actual course of events in the Scottish uplands following human occupation must have been rather similar to this hypothetical outline.

The theme of this book, therefore, is the re-appraisal of land use in a predominantly cool, wet environment of impoverished soils, where there is a general tendency towards water surpluses and peat forma-

4

tion but where localized pockets of more fertile soil and more favourable climate exist. The original climax ecosystems have long since been destroyed or, at best, persist in highly modified form. How are we to bring an ecological approach to this situation so that the potentialities of each region and each particular site can be most fully realized and at the same time conserved for a sustained yield? To some extent this sizing up of the landscape is done unconsciously by all who manage or exploit land, using their appreciation of soil, altitude, slope, exposure, aspect, and drainage, and at the same time noting the presence or absence of indicator plants and communities. The land use ecologist works in exactly the same way but takes a broader and more long-term view even than the farmer, grazier or forester.

As in practically all land use problems in the long-settled countries of the world the difficulties standing in the way of rationalization are not technical but social and economic. There is in Great Britain a fundamental lack of interest by Government in the remoter areas and the absence of any real determination to improve the situation. This country is geared to an industrial way of life and to existence in enormous 'conurbations', and consideration is given primarily to the well-being of the close-packed populations, with secondary attention to those involved in the more intensive forms of agriculture and little thought for the outer fringes. We are, however, rich in the lip service paid to the ideal of life in the harder environments and in the number and variety of reports and white papers on the problems of the uplands lying disregarded on the shelves. We now stand on the threshold of new developments and, whether or not Great Britain is admitted to membership of the European Common Market, great changes will take place in our use of the Scottish Uplands. These must be set on an ecological basis if we are to avoid a breakdown of social life outside the larger population centres.

1. *The Upland Environment*

Consideration of the ecology of land use in any area must be firmly based on the history of the area, both natural and human. This is certainly true of Scotland, and splendid accounts of Scotland's history in ecological terms have been given by Ritchie (1919), Darling (1955), Anderson (1962), and others. Only the merest summary will be given here, as an indication of the part that social, political and economic factors have played and still play in interaction with the physical environment, in forming the present ecological situation.

About 3000 BC, at the start of the Neolithic period, Scotland was heavily forested. From the beginnings of agriculture, areas of forest were cleared, first by burning, then by cutting. The more the population turned from hunting to agriculture for sustenance, the greater the clearances became. As grazing became more general, so this too required reduction of forests.

In the centuries that followed, Anglo-Saxons, Romans, and Scots from Ireland continued to clear more forest. According to traditional accounts and corroboratory charcoal layers near the surface of the peat and under the forest humus, further large tracts of the Highlands were devastated by extensive forest fires in the course of Viking and clan raids. Sheep husbandry by rich and powerful monasteries then became established in the twelfth and thirteenth centuries on the fringes of the diminished oak forests in southern Scotland.

The seventeenth century saw the start of forest clearances for commercial purposes which culminated in complete forest destruction 200 years later. Increased attention began to be paid to the more remote oak forests of the west and the pine forests of the north for boat building and iron smelting. The system of land use prevailing under the clan system at this time was probably not self-sufficient, and the maintenance of the population depended to some extent on the spoils of war brought back from outside the Highland region.

The Act of Union of 1707 provided a southern market for the black Highland cattle which were now bred as readily exportable stores in greater numbers than ever before. At the same time the increased prosperity of the larger landowners led to some attempt at restoration of the vanishing forests by amenity planting.

After 1745 a form of feudalism replaced the clan system in the Highlands and exploitation of land resources was greatly accelerated in the ensuing 'colonial' period. Southern sheep graziers spread northward to occupy much of the Highlands, from Perthshire and Argyll to Sutherland; they continued the destruction of the forest by felling, burning and barking trees, and effectively preventing most tree regeneration.

Cessation of clan warfare, followed by the introduction of the potato, led to what we should now call a population explosion in the Highlands. This was made one of the excuses for the simultaneous clearance of whole districts of their human inhabitants to make way for the encroaching Blackface and Cheviot sheep. The dispossessed people drifted south to the developing industrial areas, emigrated to America and Australia, or accepted the tiny holdings sometimes offered them along the western seaboard where they could attempt to eke out a livelihood by fishing and kelp burning. Public outcry at the inhumanity of the clearances led eventually to legal recognition by the Crofters Act of 1886 and later legislation of the right of those who remained to the tenure of their holdings.

The nineteenth century also saw the development of deer forest and grouse moor, in part replacing the earlier sheep runs, as sporting interests became fashionable among the new class of wealthy industrialist that was forming in the south. Thus, while a reduction in population is often recommended as a prerequisite for an improvement in land use, the savage depopulation of the Highlands merely ushered in an era of more extensive misuse and intensified exploitation.

In the present century two new forms of land use have taken their place alongside hill sheep farming, crofting and sporting: commercial timber growing by the State and by private landowners, and nature conservation by State and other public bodies.

ROCKS

The two basic elements in the environment of plants, animals, and man are the rocks that provide the inorganic framework of the soil and the climate under which soil and vegetation develop. Many excellent accounts of the geology of Scotland, both popular and technical, are available to the reader (for example, Geikie 1887, Phemister 1948, Read 1948, Richey 1948). For present purposes the rocks of the Scottish uplands can be grouped according to their soil-forming properties in the following way.

Lewisian gneisses. These are found in the north-west Highlands and in the Outer Hebrides and they provide some of the most inhospitable low ground in Britain. They are hard rocks and have been swept bare and polished by the ice sheets of the Pleistocene glaciation so that their undulating topography and poor drainage encourages peat formation. Sedentary soils are seldom found, and peat may be developed directly upon the bedrock or an overlying glacial till of gneissic, Torridonian sandstone or quartzitic origin. Most of the gneisses are acidic (siliceous) but there may be a few basic or calcareous bands which render the local springs and seepage water rich in minerals. Within range of these percolating waters pockets of fertile brown soil are formed.

Torridonian sandstone. This formation includes sandstone, shales and conglomerates and is confined to the north-west Highlands and the islands of Skye and Rum. The sandstones are mostly hard and the ice-smoothed bedrock is again largely peat covered. Sedentary soils are formed more readily than on Lewisian gneiss but they are easily podzolized and most are acutely deficient in nutrients. Many glacial deposits of the north-west Highlands consist of mixed gneiss and sandstone debris, densely compacted and badly drained. The shale bands may be calcareous and these give rise to local pockets of fertile soils.

Old Red Sandstone. This formation covers the same range of texture as the Torridonian, but the rocks are more porous and relatively rich in mineral nutrients so that its outcrops are generally marked by areas of cultivation. The Old Red Sandstone occurs extensively in Caithness, east Ross-shire, around Turrif, and from Fochabers to Loch Ness. Where peat cover has developed it is not deep, except on parts of the blanket bog of central Caithness, and the underlying tills can often be reclaimed quite profitably.

Metamorphic rocks of the Moine and Dalradian series. These rocks, or the glacial debris derived from them, are the prevailing rocks of the Scottish Highlands, the Moine formation to the north and west of the Dalradian. They have a wide range of mineral composition and soil-forming potential, with the acid, siliceous members in greater abundance. The quartzites are the poorest soil formers and give coarse, readily podzolized soils. The non-calcareous mica-schists give quite good sedentary soils, but they are lime-deficient. The limestones and calcareous mica-schists give the best soils but they are localized and are often covered by deep peat so that their full effect on vegetation development is lost. Water percolating through the calcareous beds may extend the influence of these rocks far beyond the area of their outcrop and may render the surrounding acid areas capable of affording good grazing. The most frequently occurring rocks of the series are granulite, slate, quartzite, siliceous and calcareous mica-schists and limestone.

Plateau basalts of Tertiary and Old Red Sandstone age. The Tertiary basalts are found in Skye, Mull, Morvern and the Small Isles, those of Old Red Sandstone age to the east of Oban. All give fine-grained, free-draining soils, but the non-calcareous members resemble the siliceous mica-schists in their ease of weathering combined with calcium de-

8

ficiency. Large areas of the outcrops are peat covered, but sedentary and deep-weathered soils are common and these give good grazing and reasonably good arable land.

Cambrian quartzite. This rock runs in a band through the north-west Highlands from Foinaven through Ben More, Assynt and Beinn Eighe to Kishorn and Skye. On both low and high ground it gives rise to barren and inhospitable country rivalling that of the Lewisian gneiss. Its soil-forming potential is similar to that of the Dalradian quartzite which it much resembles in appearance, and where the glacial debris derived from it is unmixed with other rocks a surface layer of acid raw humus and peat is inevitable. Quartzite soils are the least fertile in Scotland and the vegetation they carry is the most impoverished and susceptible to degradation.

Cambrian dolomite and mudstone. A narrow and intermittent band of these rocks accompanies the Cambrian quartzite through the north-west Highlands from Durness to Skye. Except where peat covered they give rise to pockets of reddish-brown, fertile and sometimes calcareous loam at all elevations. On the low ground they may be under cultivation, as in the crofting townships of Elphin and Cnocan, but they are mostly marked by a heavily grazed, grassy and mossy sward among the brown expanses of heather, deer hair sedge, and cotton grass moorland.

Granite intrusions. The acid, igneous rocks, of which granite is the principal representative, are not regional in their occurrence like the formations so far dealt with. The main granite intrusions of the Highlands are to be found in Caithness, in the Cairngorm and Aberdeen areas, Rannoch Moor, Loch Etive, and Kingairloch. In the Southern Uplands there is an important granite mass in Central Galloway. Granite, syenite and diorite all give rise to coarse, free draining and acid soils, leaching readily but not as impoverished of mineral nutrients as the quartzite and Torridonian sandstone soils. The outcrops are commonly peat covered on the low ground and the larger granite areas influence extensive tracts of the surrounding country through the glacial debris they have produced.

Basic and ultra-basic intrusions. Gabbros, peridotites and other less common basic and ultra-basic rocks occur in the Cuillins of Skye, in Rum, in Ardnamurchan and in Aberdeenshire. They are hard rocks, scoured clean by the ice in the west and often peat covered. They may be deeply weathered like the softer basalts to give sedentary soils similar to those of the non-calcareous and fine grained basic rocks and, like them, rich in iron oxides. Cultivated and grazing lands on the ultra-basics may produce problems of toxicity to animals through excess of minor elements accumulated in the vegetation.

Liassic and Cretaceous rocks. Rocks of these formations are found in small patches protected by the basalt flows of Raasay, Skye, Mull, and the Small Isles. They are soft and often calcareous so that they give rise to excellent agricultural soils when on level ground. Outcrops on steep slopes give rich pasture which is generally overgrazed at all times of year and shows various stages of erosion.

Ordovician and Silurian rocks of the Southern Uplands. This important series of mudstones, shales, grits and greywackes, with some volcanic rocks, does not differ greatly from the Moine and Dalradian metamorphic series in chemical composition, but the rocks are softer and more easily weathered to give fine grained soils. Peat formation and gleying are common features and the mineral soils of steep slopes show much sheet washing and gully erosion under the prevailing hill sheep regime.

SOILS

The soils developed from these rocks and their glacial products are mostly young, and began to form after the retreat of the last ice sheets and glaciers some 12,000 to 15,000 years ago. The range of climates under which they were developed does not appear to have differed greatly from the climate of the present day, although frost patterned soils of the mountains, which are no longer being actively sorted, indicate a colder, late glacial period. Certain red-brown basalt and limestone soils must have been developed under warmer conditions, either in pre-glacial times escaping subsequent ice erosion or during the post-glacial climatic optimum. These soils can be grouped quite roughly from the vegetation and land use point of view; the principal groups are as follows:

Alluvial and meadow soils. These are developed on flat land bordering lochs and rivers and formerly carried a vegetation of marshland and alder wood. They may be waterlogged permanently or seasonally unless artificially drained for agriculture.

Acid brown forest soils. These soils bear a superficial resemblance to the true brown earths, which are rare in Scotland and possess greater reserves of fertility. Nevertheless, the acid brown soils are some of the most fertile of the uplands.

Yellow-brown podzolic soils (cryptopodzolic brown earths). Sometimes formerly described as 'truncated podzols' because of their resemblance to the B-horizon or subsoil of certain podzols, this group is particularly characteristic of birch woods and vegetation derived from them. They possess an intermediate level of fertility among the soils of the uplands and are particularly common in eastern regions.

Podzols and gley podzols. There are several varieties of podzols, some with well-developed surface peat layer and some with a distinct iron or humus cemented layer in the subsoil. All have a low level of fertility.

Skeletal mineral soils. These are found on steep slopes, especially at higher altitudes, and consist essentially of finely divided rock intermixed with a little humus and undecomposed plant debris. Podzolization has not proceeded far and, consequently, such soils have an intermediate fertility level.

Reddish-brown limestone loams. Limestone soils are of smaller extent than the area of outcrop of the parent rocks would suggest. It is doubtful if they could be developed under the existing climate and they appear to be relics from an earlier, warmer period. They are extremely fertile.

Alpine humus soils. These are the most fertile of the soils developed above the potential forest limit. They are not unlike skeletal soils with much acid humus incorporated in the surface layers, but there is no development of pure raw humus.

Hill peats. This term covers a wide range of peat depth beyond the point at which living plant roots still make contact with the underlying mineral horizons. Many are essentially podzols with a strongly developed surface peat layer. Deep peat may also be developed directly upon bedrock.

The agricultural soils of the uplands come mainly from alluvials, acid brown soils and podzolics. The best rough grazing is found on alluvials, skeletal soils and uncultivated patches of acid brown soils and podzols. The bulk of the hill grazings are found on podzolics and deep peats.

The harder acid rocks give rise to mineral soils, rather than a cover of deep peat, only where their glacial or fluvio-glacial derivatives have acted as the parent material. The softer acid rocks may develop peat-free sedentary mineral soils. Peats may form directly upon any hard bedrock, even limestone.

The acid rocks predominating in the Scottish uplands give rise to soils with a low content of available plant nutrients so that soils with fertility of agricultural standards are strictly localized. In the cool, wet climate of these regions podzolization is the principal soil-forming process, and this downward movement of iron and aluminium ions is accompanied by an accumulation of raw humus in the surface soil horizons. Naturally fertile soils are maintained largely by irrigation with water which is strongly charged with minerals removed from relatively basic rocks in the course of percolation and partly by mechanical instability under the action of gravity, frost, and running surface water, all of which counteract the leaching process.

A readily available supply of calcium is the most important factor in bringing about and maintaining floristic richness in the upland vegetation. The number of plant species pre ent can thus provide a clue to palatability and nutritional value of the forage, a wide variety of grasses and other herbs indicating valuable grazing. The converse does not necessarily hold good, and calcium differences too small to be reflected in the variety of vegetation may be significant for the grazing animals, which certainly seek out those areas where soil calcium is above average.

Availability of the element phosphorus is important from both the plant and animal point of view. Differences in the soil phosphorus level are not generally reflected in vegetation composition in the uplands, however, except in so far as this runs parallel to the calcium level (but see p. 48).

CLIMATE

The climate of the Scottish uplands is cool, temperate, and oceanic, but within this generalization lie numerous local climates of greater severity culminating in that endured by the highest summits—which can best be described as oceanic-subarctic. Numerous accounts of the British climate are available, containing detailed discussion of each of the climatic factors in turn (for example, Green 1964, Manley 1952). The latest and most ecological in approach is that of Green. In these accounts stress is generally laid upon the equability of temperature, the general cloudiness and lack of bright sunshine, the prevalence of strong winds, high humidity and moderate to high rainfall. This makes a reasonable summary for many purposes.

Considering its high latitude of 56-59° north, Scotland possesses some anomalous climatic features. These stem from the warm, enveloping North Atlantic ocean currents and the regional atmospheric circulation, which maintains a cool or mild maritime air stream over the country at most times of year. As a result of this, the southern Outer Hebrides have a long frost-free period from the end of March or the beginning of April to early December, whereas the glens of the eastern Highlands are less favoured and can count on the absence of frost only from about mid-June to mid-August. Elevated plateaux in the east are liable to frost at any time of year.

The length of the growing season for crop plants, measured in the standard way as accumulation of day degrees Fahrenheit above a 43°F threshold (or day degrees Centigrade above a 6°C threshold) varies from zero in the mountains to 2,500 in the most favoured coastal areas. However, many wild plants, especially those that grow in the mountains, have a lower growth threshold than this.

Because of the small amplitude of the diurnal and annual temperature fluctuations, the normal fall in temperature with increasing altitude (one F degree for each 300 ft or one C degree for each 50 m) assumes greater importance than in continental climates. Coupled with the increase in rainfall and exposure to wind that is experienced with increasing altitude, this gives height above sea level great importance for both plants and animals in the upland environment. In the Outer Hebrides the average annual wind speed exceeds 18 m.p.h. and the average annual number of days with gale force winds (in excess of 38 m.p.h.) exceeds thirty. Records kept on the summit of Ben Nevis 4,406 ft (1,322 m) over a period of sixteen years indicated an average of 261 gales each year.

The wettest part of the region lies inland from the west coast, with rainfall exceeding 150 ins (3,750 mm) in Lochaber and Knoydart, the rain falling on more than 250 days of the year. By way of contrast, the shores of the Moray Firth may receive a total of only 22 ins (550 mm), falling on 180 days. The extra wetness of the west is experienced mainly during the winter months.

The frequency of occurrence of hill fog at any site is roughly proportional to the elevation. Fog reduces temperature and light intensity as well as maintaining high air humidity; its incidence is therefore important in any consideration of altitudinal vegetation zonation along with the other factors of temperature, wind speed and so on.

That unequal snow cover as a result of wind drifting is important in determining vegetation patterns was first emphasized by European plant sociologists. Poore and McVean (1957) and McVean (1958) showed that this factor influenced vegetation composition in the oceanic Scottish Highlands as well as in more continental climates.

Within recent years greater attention has been paid in Britain to the evaporating power of the atmosphere at any site, in relation to the rainfall experienced there, as a means of summing all the elements of the climate from the point of view of plant growth. This can be done by calculating from climatic records, or by determining directly the potential water loss by evaporation and transpiration from a grass sward, and comparing this with the actual rainfall. Potential water surpluses and deficits can then be calculated and, since these depend upon both incoming solar radiation and rainfall, they provide a useful single figure for the ecologist. Growing season in daydegrees, precipitation: evaporation ratios, and various indices of oceanicity have attempted to fulfil the same function but are less generally applicable.

Green has described the procedure for determining potential evapotranspiration by direct measurement (1963) and has prepared an interim map of the British Isles showing the distribution of potential water deficits and surpluses (1964). The boundary between places with significant potential water deficits and those without any is an

13

important phytogeographic dividing line. Green's map shows that a large area in the west Highlands has no significant water deficit, and this area corresponds to the region of blanket peat formation on steep slopes and level ground alike (figure 1). The dividing line rises from sea level in the west to about 2,000 ft (600 m) in the Cairngorm area, so that only the highest ground of the east-central Highlands and central Galloway give outliers of the region without a potential water deficit. At the other extreme, places along the eastern seaboard give values of potential water deficit rising to about three inches per year. In south-eastern England there is a maximum potential water deficit of about six inches (150 mm).

It must be emphasized that more detailed records would show a more complicated pattern than this, with many small pockets of potential water deficit within the western area of potential surplus. These pockets may be found to coincide with the coastal patches of cultivation and brown mineral soils, although any exact correspondence will be complicated by the local geology and the human history of the area.

In conclusion, Green (1964) has pointed out that relatively minor changes in atmospheric circulation over the British Isles can alter completely the average seasonal distribution of rainfall in relation to potential evaporation and hence bring about profound ecological changes.

WATER SUPPLIES

The Scottish system of rivers and lochs, particularly in the Highland areas, is intricate, and the terrain is generally well watered. A striking feature of the Highland system is the nearness of the watershed to the west coast so that the westward flowing streams are short and have some of the characteristics of torrents (a river flow marked by sharp flood peaks), while those flowing to the east are much longer and have a greater proportion of level, carse land in their middle and lower reaches.

Another feature of the Highland rivers is the substantial area of peat covered land (much of it deep peat) in the catchments. The proportion of bare rock is also high, especially in the catchments of the westward flowing streams. Since rainfall is generally high and well distributed much of the peat cover remains saturated for long periods and may develop an impermeable skin which readily sheds precipitation. This feature is discussed in the sections on moor burning and erosion. Saturated or impermeable peat and bare rock together produce a flashy

---

Figure 1. Areas with and without potential water deficit in Scotland.

3 – 6 in (75 – 150 mm)	
0·5 – 3 in (12·5 – 75 mm)	
< 0·5 in (12·5 mm)	

river flow with sharp flood peaks. Features which tend to alleviate this, such as continuous winter snow accumulation, forest cover, and actively growing bog surfaces, are now largely lacking in the Scottish uplands, the first as the result of climatic amelioration, the last two as a result of human activities. Coincidence of rapid snow melt at all levels and violent rain storms may produce severe flooding in the first few months of the year. On the other hand, exceptionally cold winters may still lock up temporarily a high proportion of the precipitation and reduce winter run off from the higher ranges.

As explained in a later chapter, moor burning must take most of the blame for the inactivation of bog surfaces and the production of an impermeable surface on most peat lands. The development of powerful drainage machinery has led to a substantial increase in the number of drains being cut in connection with hill sheep and cattle husbandry. This hardly affects the water storage capacity of the peat but it does lead to quicker run off. The preparation of peat ground for afforestation has a similar effect but it should only be temporary as the closure of the tree canopy will restore an even better regulation of run off than existed prior to the drainage.

In spite of the fact that these repeatedly burned and eroding peat lands behave hydrologically like any other eroding soil, flood peaks of the rivers are not remarkable when compared with those of other countries and destructive floods are comparatively rare. There is, however, a suspicion that damaging floods have been recurring with greater frequency over the last few decades, a phenomenon which cannot be attributed to the occurrence of heavier rain storms. For example, there have been the Berwickshire floods of 1948 and floods in the White Esk–Ettrick, Dulnan, and Lochaber areas in 1953—as well as numerous smaller examples of cloudburst damage in 1947, 1949, 1955 and 1963 in Skye, Sutherland, and the Cairngorms. In fact, locally damaging floods occur in some part of the country practically every year, but they seldom recur in the same watershed at intervals of less than 20-50 years.

During damaging storms large quantities of debris may be removed from the banks of streams towards their headwaters and new gullies are formed on the surrounding hillsides. This debris increases the erosive force of the river downstream and the transported material is spread out in cones and sheets, sometimes over land of agricultural value. The channel of the main river is unable to hold the increased flow, alluvial flats are flooded, roads and bridges swept away, and there may be heavy losses among farm stock.

There is also some evidence that recent floods have adversely affected stream beds for spawning and feeding of trout and salmon. The

16

suspended peat in many flood waters is also harmful to the young stages of these fish through its interference with gill action.

One of the symptoms of deterioration in the uniformity of river flow has been the loss to cultivation of substantial areas of formerly reclaimed carse land, notably along the Spey between Kincraig and Ruthven. A prolonged enquiry (Speyside Drainage Report, unpublished) has recently found that a second reclamation of this ground would be quite uneconomic at the present day, so that agriculture's loss is a gain for the wildlife of Strathspey.

While Scottish river floods are seldom spectacular, the nadir flows give greater cause for anxiety, although they attract less attention. Flows are commonly at their minimum during the period of spring anticyclones, which may dominate British weather at any time from March to June, and in some years may be prolonged. Agricultural, industrial, and domestic water supplies are all affected, fish stocks suffer from the concentration of any pollution and the decreased oxygen content of the water, and estuaries may become badly fouled. Hydroelectric systems, which allow large volumes of water to escape unutilized in time of flood, may be reduced to working considerably under peak capacity and workers may have to be laid off. This is a common occurrence at the British Aluminium Company's factory at Fort William (Turnock, 1966).

Fraser Darling, in his West Highland Survey (1955), has drawn attention to the sensitivity of the ostensibly well-watered Highlands to drought, especially in spring after a hard winter and before the vegetation has begun to grow. Deforestation and moor burning must again bear the blame. Intact forest, scrub and bog can do much to buffer climatic extremes. Most forest and moorland fires occur during the periods of high evapotranspiration and they, in their turn, aggravate the harmful effects of subsequent droughts. The fodder situation for both wild animals and domestic stock can be critical in those years when prolonged snow cover and low temperatures are followed immediately by the driest, sunniest weather of the year.

Vegetation

Grassland, dwarf shrub heaths, and various types of wet moorland and bog constitute the greater part of the upland vegetation of Scotland. Forest, both natural and planted, moss heaths on the highest ground, and the rare, herb-dominated patches of late snow fields and inaccessible mountain ledges make up the remainder. Surviving native woodland and scrub is generally thin so that the trees and bushes have little effect on the subordinate species which thus show much the same groupings as in the vegetation outside the woodland limits.

17

It has been pointed out that the majority of the upland soils are acid, wet, and peaty, with many thoroughly and deeply leached mineral soils capped with raw humus. The vegetation accompanying these soils is dominated by acidophilous species, in which a small number of grasses, sedges, and shrubs comprise the great bulk of the plant communities.

Below a level of about 2,800 ft (840 m) heather, with or without the two common cotton grasses, is the most prominent species in the central and eastern Highlands, so that it dominates the physiognomy of moorland and bog alike. In the western Highlands and in the Southern Uplands, *Molinia* grass, deer hair sedge, cotton grass, bent, and fescue oust the heather from its dominant position, and any one of these may be locally the most abundant species although a mixture of several of them, together with stunted heather, is a common type of cover. Bracken occupies much free-draining mineral soil or thin, dry peat.

Above 2,700 ft (810 m) blaeberry–crowberry heaths, moss heaths and *Nardus* grassland occupy most of the ground. All three vary considerably, according to the lime content of the underlying rock, in nutritive value for grazing animals. Rocks rich in lime, vegetation rich in species, and high nutritive value of the plants generally go together.

More detailed descriptions of the regional vegetational pattern will be found in Burnett (1964), Darling and Boyd (1964), and McVean and Ratcliffe (1962). The most significant vegetation types of these regions from the land use point of view will now be described.

WOODLAND

1. Pinewood with tall heather and blaeberry and thick moss. The pines are usually widely spaced. In the drier eastern woods and wherever the trees are closer together heather is largely eliminated and *Sphagnum* disappears from the moss mixture, leaving a blaeberry and feather moss community which is also found in the older pine plantations. (plate 1). The densest woods and plantations have a moss and litter covered floor in which even the blaeberry is sparse.

2. Birchwood with short blaeberry and abundant moss. This is close to the blaeberry and feather moss pinewoods but contains a greater variety of species on what is generally a finer textured and more fertile soil.

3. Birch or oak wood with mossy and grassy floor, containing some broad-leaved herbs and blaeberry. In this type of woodland the variety of species is greater than in the first two and the soil is generally a yellow-brown podzolic or acid brown forest soil. These woods provide good grazing (plates 2, 3, and 4).

4. Pure heather sward with a sparse growth of mosses and lichens. This is heather moor in the strict sense, virtually a monoculture maintained by fire. It sustains high grouse populations and provides some grazing for sheep and deer (plate 5).

5. Damp heather moor with blaeberry, crowberry and much deep moss. Pure heather moor tends to develop into this community type if unburned for about 50 years. It is extremely close floristically to the more open pinewoods, and is commonly found on north-facing slopes and at higher altitudes in the eastern Highlands or replacing pure heather moor at all levels in the west.

6. Dwarf heather sward with a variety of other dwarf shrubs and lichens. This is an extension of pure heather moor above 2,000 ft (600 m), but it is not so amenable to management due to the slower growth of the heather and the dwarf habit of all the constituent plants. It contains a greater number and variety of berry-bearing species than pure heather moor, especially in the northern Highlands. A variant found in the west and north-west is rich in *Rhacomitrium* moss and is of much less value for either domestic animals or wild life.

BLAEBERRY HEATHS

7. Blaeberry heath with few other species or with crowberry and much moss. These are found at the higher levels on the hills where snow accumulates and lies late on northern and eastern faces. Being often under winter snow they have little significance as grazing at that time of year and even in summer they provide little to attract the grazing animal.

8. Blaeberry heath with a few grasses and sedges and abundant lichens. This occurs in some districts where there are softer, calcareous rocks and it may be found on quite exposed ground. Grazing can take place almost throughout the year, the fodder being provided mostly by grasses in summer and dwarf shrubs in winter.

9. Blaeberry heath rich in fescue and alpine lady's mantle. This type is confined to the most calcareous rocks of the southern Highlands and, being comparatively rich in species, provides a better quality grazing than the other blaeberry heaths. There is again a *Rhacomitrium* variant in the north-west Highlands, inferior in floristic composition and grazing value.

10. Crowberry heaths with much Rhacomitrium moss. These can be included in this group because all transitions from them to the poorer types of blaeberry heath are found. This is a west Highland heath, mainly of high-lying boulder slopes. With the exception of a few berries it produces little for domestic stock or wild life and it contains few plant species.

11. and 12. Bent–fescue grassland (11) with few species; and (12) with a variety of species. These two grasslands constitute the best of the un-improved upland grazings. They are developed on mineral soils, generally on steepish slopes, and are characteristic of certain geological formations such as calcareous schist, basalt, some sandstones, and other easily-weathered rocks. The species-poor grasslands may have slightly peaty soils but they are free-draining and provide useful summer grazing.

Both types are widespread in certain districts of the southern and western Highlands and in the Southern Uplands, but the more species-rich grasslands and the poor grasslands rich in alpine lady's mantle are always localized and confined to the more calcareous rocks so that there is a tendency for them to suffer from too continuous and close grazing. The grazing season is generally short, especially at the higher levels, but they may provide some keep for animals in an open winter.

13. and 14. Nardus grassland of the sub-alpine zone; Juncus squarrosus 'grassland' of the sub-alpine zone. These types can be considered together in the same way as the bent–fescue grasslands because they have certain features in common, although one is dominated by a grass and the other by a rush. Both dominants provide only the poorest grazing but the subordinate species are more valuable and the dominants may be eaten in spring before anything else is available. They occur on peats with a wide range of mineral status according to the local rocks so that the poorer examples have few accompanying species while the richer ones have a wide variety of grasses and other herbs of good feeding value. The best examples are found in Breadalbane and along the outcrop of the Dalradian limestone.

15. Mixed grassland of peat podzols and acid, peaty gleys in which abundant *Deschampsia flexuosa* and *Nardus* or *Molinia* occur along with the bent and fescue. These are typical of the upper slopes of the Southern Uplands below the level of the blanket peat and are closely related to type *11*.

16. Mixed grasslands of poorly drained soils in which abundant *Molinia* and *Deschampsia caespitosa* occur with bent and fescue. These are again frequent on the Southern Uplands below an altitude of 1,250 ft (375 m), and are more closely related to types *13* and *14* than to alpine *D. caespitosa* grassland.

17. Bent–fescue grassland with Poa pratensis developed in localized patches where sheep lie up at night or where seabirds congregate on maritime swards.

18. Alpine Deschampsia caespitosa grassland with species-rich and species-poor variants. These are less widespread than the other grasslands but they have some similarities to the higher examples of type *14*. Once again species-poor examples are to be found on siliceous rocks and species-rich stands, which provide quite good grazing, on calcareous rocks. They have a wide altitudinal range and can be found up to 4,000 ft (1,200 m).

19. Molinia grasslands, with or without bog myrtle. The *Molinia* grasslands cover a wide range of soil composition and wetness related to those of types *15* and *16*; the less valuable examples constitute one of the principal grazing communities of the west Highlands and Southern Uplands. Where lime-rich water emerges from the bedrock or glacial till the *Molinia* itself makes a nutritious fodder in early summer and the many accompanying species are of value throughout the season. Bog myrtle will be eaten by red deer when they are verging on starvation.

The peats formed from *Molinia* are well humified, largely amorphous, and of relatively high mineral status. On being drained they provide a good soil for the faster growing conifers.

20. Nardus grasslands of the low and middle alpine zones (2,000-4,000 ft; 600-1,200 m). These grasslands are developed where there is a fairly persistent cover of winter snow so that, apart from their limited grazing value, they are generally unavailable from December to April or May. In general, the subsidiary species are less valuable for grazing than those of the *Nardus* grasslands at lower levels, partly because of the lower mineral status of the soil. Mosses and lichens enter into the composition of the vegetation to a greater extent.

21. Carex bigelowii heaths with much moss. Like the high-lying *Nardus* grasslands these sedge communities are often covered by snow for several months of the year. The dominant sedge is grazed, but mosses are often the most prominent element in the vegetation.

22. Juncus trifidus heaths with sparse grasses, broad-leaved herbs and lichens. These heaths occupy the most exposed ground in the Scottish mountains so that they are not favoured for grazing except during brief spells of calm weather in the summer months. They have nothing to offer for three-quarters of the year, but during the months of June, July, and August they do provide small quantities of fescue and other palatable grasses and small herbs. The vegetation is open, covering less than 20 per cent of the ground, so that the total production is small.

MOSS HEATHS

23. Rhacomitrium moss heaths, both species-rich and species-poor. Moss heaths are the characteristic vegetation of the high tops just as heather moor is of the low ground. They are almost as exposed as the *Juncus* heaths and, like them, have a short productive season. The same limited range of palatable species, such as sheep's fescue and sedges, is present, but the soil is usually more peaty. Species-rich stands are rare and of small extent on outcrops of calcareous rocks in the northern Highlands and Breadalbane; in these the variety of grasses and mountain herbs is much greater and they provide valuable grazing locally, if only for a short period of the year.

24. *Rhytidiadelphus moss heaths, with Deschampsia caespitosa,* both species-rich and species-poor. These heaths, since they occupy more sheltered ground than *Rhacomitrium* heath, are more often snow covered in winter. The species-poor variant has probably the same low grazing value as the poor *Rhacomitrium* heath, with the coarse grass, *D. caespitosa,* replacing sedges to some extent; but the variant rich in species, which is found on the steep sides of corries, probably makes better grazing than the rich *Rhacomitrium* heath owing to the greater luxuriance of the vegetation in the more sheltered site.

25. *Late snow bed moss heaths with dwarf willow (Salix herbacea).* Vegetation of these longest-lasting snow beds is included for the sake of completing the range of vegetation types to be found in the Scottish mountains, but the total area they occupy is minute. Such vegetation is exposed for only about three months of the year at most and they may not be exposed at all after a snowy winter. Mosses are nearly always the dominant species and vascular plants are few and scattered.

BOGS

26. *Cotton grass – deer hair sedge bog,* with or without other sedges and bog myrtle. This type of bog can also be called western blanket bog since it is the prevailing one in western and north-western Scotland at low levels. It is best developed in western Ross-shire and in Sutherland where it forms large tracts of 'flowe' country. The vegetation is not luxuriant except in local patches that receive natural irrigation, and even the best adapted species, such as deer hair sedge, suffer from mineral deficiencies.

The underlying peat is compact and colloidal, and undergoes irreversible changes on thorough drying to give a dark, granular substance which is a good medium for tree growth when the phosphorus deficiency has been corrected. The bog itself responds well to fertilizing and reseeding without other treatment, the introduced grasses and clovers then growing in a sort of water culture with the peat and surface turf providing little more than mechanical support.

27. *Cotton grass – heather bog* (including cotton grass – crowberry bog at high levels). This is the typical bog of eastern Scotland, but it can also be found in the west at higher levels than the previous type. The variant in which crowberry replaces heather is found only above about 2,500 ft (750 m).

The underlying peat is fibrous and stringy and may contain poorly humified *Sphagnum* layers. Gully erosion, often in a complex pattern, is practically universal since this bog is included with other heathery vegetation in any programme of periodic burning. The burning tends to eliminate heather in favour of cotton grass and the end product of the change can be seen in the blanket bogs of the English Pennines.

In contrast to the western bog there is less response, or none, to phosphate fertilizer, and direct seeding is a more difficult operation. The cotton grass, *Eriophorum vaginatum*, provides valuable grazing in early spring when other species have hardly begun growth.

28. Deer hair sedge–heather moor, rich in either mosses or lichens. This type of vegetation forms the transition between 'moor' (drier) and 'bog' (wetter), and between the vegetation of shallow and deep peat respectively. It is rather eastern in its distribution and is regularly burned; indeed it may owe its origin almost entirely to changes in the peat surface of pure heather moor caused by repeated burning under the more humid conditions of higher altitudes or locally poorer drainage.

29. Molinia–heather moor. This is the western equivalent of the deer hair sedge–heather moor and, like it, has probably been developed by periodic burning of more heather-rich vegetation in a high rainfall area. The grazing value is rather greater, particularly in early summer when the *Molinia* is sprouting.

The peat composition varies between fibrous and amorphous depending on the relative amounts of heather and *Molinia* and the wetness of the site.

30. Rush and sedge bogs with Sphagnum or brown mosses. A wide range of wet ground communities can be included here. The stands are localized but are often significant from the grazing point of view, especially where the damp hollows that contain them are the only spots in the area where mineral-rich water is concentrated. An early cut of bog hay from these sites used to be a valuable addition to the winter fodder supplies of hill farms.

2. *Geological and Accelerated Erosion of Soil and Peat*

In the British Isles the even distribution of rainfall allows the farmer to take considerable liberties with soil cultivation, and signs of erosion on arable land are exceptional. In a dry spring it is still possible to observe topsoil blowing in clouds from newly harrowed fields in eastern districts, and sheet wash with incipient gullying of exposed soil on steep slopes is common during heavy rain storms. But, on the whole, the traveller familiar with the catastrophic erosion that can be seen, for example, in North America or the Indian sub-continent will come across little in these islands to alarm him.

It is in the upland areas of this country that the erosion problems lie, and even the eye trained in the recognition of danger signs in semi-arid lands may well fail to recognize the extent of the damage here. Although there are quite noticeable gullies, landslips, and bare slopes, these are liable to be dismissed as natural phenomena and debited to an environmental severity which is not really primary but has been brought about by the very processes of deforestation and burning which have produced the erosion. Less spectacular evidence is entirely overlooked because it does not quite resemble the picture in the text books.

The distinction between 'geological' and 'accelerated' erosion can be rather fine at higher elevations, and a feature which starts as a result of human activity may develop into something indistinguishable from surrounding, but milder, geological phenomena. It is also common to find a basically geological erosion feature rendered malignant by the treatment of the surroundings. Unless expensive man-made structures are threatened by slides and gullies it is generally out of the question to contemplate direct control on land of low productivity. This, however, does not preclude attempts to prevent such occurrences wherever they seem to be impending.

The most effective and least expensive action that can be taken in countering erosion is preventive. Yet, even where the necessity for action may be agreed, the expense, in the form of reduced returns from the land over a possibly prolonged period, may be regarded as prohibitive by the user.

What, first of all, are the symptoms of accelerated erosion in upland Scotland? They may be listed and classified in the following way.
Sheet erosion
Sheet washing of peats or mineral soil on moderate slopes;

Sheet erosion of moderate to deep peat on gentle slopes;
Scree formation and extension on steep slopes with shallow soil or peat.

Gully erosion

Gully formation in mineral soil or glacial till on moderate to steep slopes;
Gully erosion of deepish peat on gentle slopes.

Miscellaneous

Landslips of various kinds (classification complex);
'Bunker' erosion of deep peat or mineral soil on moderate slopes caused by animal rubbing. Associated with sheet wash;
River bank erosion;
Wind erosion of machair land.

SHEET EROSION

Sheet washing. The progress of sheet wash on pure peat is insidious and may go undetected for many years. In the early stages its occurrence is intermittent, being active in the years immediately following a fire and quiescent as plant cover returns. Each burn increases the amount of bare peat visible. Among the early signs of erosion are the appearance of hummocks around *Scirpus*, *Eriophorum* and *Erica* plants due to undercutting by wind and rain, the appearance of temporary pools after rain, and the formation of bare, lichen-crusted patches of peat not colonized by higher plants in the interval between fires.

The peat may suffer some combustion during the fire, or wet oxidation between fires, as well as from the same types of erosion as a mineral soil. Peat may continue to smoulder long after the vegetation has been burnt, leaving large bare areas depressed below the general level which may collect water during rain. These water-collecting pans suffer from frost heaving and from wind and water scour so that they are colonized only with difficulty by plants of any kind, and the way is open for the development of gullying (hagging).

Where bedrock or glacial boulders break the surface of the peat each successive fire causes some shrinkage of the peat away from the rock. Rocks just below the surface become bared and, in boulder-strewn ground, the proportion of exposed rock may increase rapidly after each fire. Rock surfaces which have just emerged from the peat have a characteristic bleached appearance not unlike that resulting from the removal of rock lichen cover by fire.

Sheet erosion. Extensive sheet erosion is seldom seen on pure heather moor unless there has been gross mismanagement or a severe accidental burn, but it is the normal state of affairs on deer hair sedge–heather moor and the drier cotton grass–heather moors (plates 5, 6 and 7).

On mineral soils sheet wash is commonest on podzols with a thin organic horizon and on the richer brown soils or limestone loams. On podzols burning is again the sole cause of the erosion; the pale, leached horizon is quickly exposed and the underlying yellow or reddish brown 'B horizon' appears in places. On the brown soils with mull humus, overgrazing, with consequent weakening of the grass turf, is generally to blame. Local overgrazing is especially liable to occur where there are limited outcrops of calcareous rocks and the grazing is uncontrolled. The animals are then free to concentrate on the more palatable and nutritious herbage of the limestone. If the underlying rock is loose and shattered, or where the 'C horizon' consists of loosely compacted till, gully erosion is likely to follow quickly upon sheet wash. This is demonstrated particularly well in Glen Tilt (plate 8).

The greater the altitude the greater the liability to erosion since vegetation is slower to recover from damage, and the action of wind, rain, and frost is accentuated. Examples of mineral soil wash may be seen at the higher levels in granite areas throughout the Scottish uplands and on the Durness limestone at Inchnadamph.

The extent to which soils are exposed to frost action, especially at the higher elevations, is not generally appreciated in this country. The lifting action of needle ice below the soil surface is an important factor in impoverished mineral soils and peats. These are only slowly colonized by vegetation during the frost-free period of the year and are thus exposed to erosion for longer than the more fertile soils.

There is no fundamental distinction between sheet washing on shallow and deep peats. Slopes with deep peat are generally less steep so that erosion is less easily started but, once initiated, it is just as persistent and the results as devastating (plate 9). Sheet wash is more often associated with gullying on the deeper peats and large areas of eroding peat may be difficult to assign to either category.

Screes. Screes are a natural part of the scene in many mountain areas, particularly at the higher levels. At low altitudes screes tend to become stabilized and overgrown with vegetation and eventually covered with a layer of soil, but in cool, wet climates with siliceous rocks this is a slow process and the soil cover may be little more than a thin layer of moss and raw humus, which is easily damaged. Except where there has been a recent rock fall or mass movement within the scree the edges of the loose rock area should show advancing tongues of vegetation. Re-activation and extension of the screes by bad land use is shown by marginal patches of bare soil or peat, or an abrupt edge to both soil and vegetation. This is more frequently the result of combined burning and grazing, only occasionally of grazing and trampling alone. Where the stones are covered by only a thin layer of moss and a sparse growth of dwarf shrubs the vegetation dries out readily in spring, and one fire is sufficient to set back the course of succession to the bare rock stage once again. Stabilized screes with a good cover of soil or peat and thick vegetation can be re-activated by one or two injudicious burnings followed by unrestricted stocking. The whole slope may become so unstable that lower down the slope loose stones cover the vegetation which was not damaged by the fire.

Scree formation and re-activation is one of the most widespread signs of erosion in Scotland and can be seen in practically every steep-sided glen (plates 5 and 7). The slopes of the Drumochter Pass and of the Ross-shire Glen Docharty may be cited as examples. Screes often have steep faces of bedrock immediately above them and torrents pouring down these faces during rain storms may cut gullies in even the most free-draining rock debris.

GULLY EROSION

Gully formation is one of the most spectacular signs of erosion, both geological and accelerated. The form of gullies is manifold, both in shape of cross-section and in ground pattern. In this country we are largely concerned with short, simple or seldom-branching gullies of broad U or V shaped cross-section in coarse, stony glacial debris. The majority of the gullies are caused primarily by the management of the catchment area above them in a way which increases the rate of run off, but weakening of the vegetation cover at the site of the gully itself is a contributory factor (plates 8, 10 and 11).

The burning of vegetation on bog catchments, the excavation of drains for pastoral and silvicultural purposes, and ploughing for afforestation are all liable to induce gullying downstream. In the gullied area, burning of heathery vegetation or the overgrazing of a grass sward tend to aggravate the erosion.

Admittedly, the occasional formation of new gullies, following exceptional rain storms, is a natural part of the upland scene. In the natural landscape at low and middle altitudes trees and shrubs quickly colonize the scars, which become stabilized and blend with the background once again. In a deforested landscape subjected to burning and grazing the scars, once formed, are there to stay, and they generally extend and become more prominent as animals range over the disturbed ground, picking off the shoots of colonizing plants and keeping the stones and soil on the move.

On the predominantly grassy slopes of the schist hills, where the glacial till and derived soils have a higher clay content, gullies often start from patches of rotational slipping or from mud-flows where a sudden excess of seepage water has burst out of the hillside. Others begin where surface water, concentrated down a bare rock face, meets the glacial till or colluvial slope below. This phenomenon can be seen from some distance away on the north-west slopes of the Lomond Hills in Kinross-shire.

The Tertiary basalt country of the west Highlands is especially liable to gullying, and the deep basalt soils over deeply weathered bedrock offer little resistance once the surface vegetation mat has been broken. The same applies in granite country where there is much unconsolidated glacial debris.

At the foot of each gully there is usually a debris cone, often covering vegetation that was of greater grazing value than that of the slope above and most often covering an alluvial grassland. Where the gully discharges directly into the main stream the debris is transported and deposited elsewhere.

Only a small proportion of the open drains of hill farms and forest land start off serious scouring which ends as active gullies, in spite of the fact that so much of the ploughing and draining is carried out directly downslope. For this the farmers and foresters have to thank the general compaction and cohesion of the underlying till. Insufficient care has been exercised in applying normal drainage procedure to areas with uncompacted sands and gravels with the result that quite spectacular wash-outs can be seen in a few places, for example near Achnasheen in Ross-shire. A greater appreciation of the local drift geology is required in all hill ploughing and drainage schemes— and also in some major road improvement schemes such as the recent work (1962–3) between Roy Bridge and Loch Laggan.

Bog bursts or flows, in which peat areas become so charged with rain water that rupture of the surface vegetation mat occurs, followed by sliding or flowing of the semi-liquid peat mass, are not considered here as they can be regarded as natural phenomena. In any case they do not seem to occur as often as they once did, probably because of the spread of peat drainage and other interference with bog surfaces. Erosion of deep peat is considered on pages 30-2.

MISCELLANEOUS

Landslips. In the classification of landslips three major types of movement are recognized: falling; slumping; sliding.

Rock, earth, and debris falls occur naturally in rugged topography. They do not normally occur as a result of bad land use (but see river bank erosion, p. 29). Slumping, with rotational movement about a horizontal axis, is common on hillsides with heavy clay soils, and especially where rainfall is high. The slump may be measurable in square yards or it may extend to several acres. It is characterized by a vertical wall at the head, where rupture of the surface took place, a central smooth area of the original surface now at a lower level, and an irregular bottom portion where the original surface is thrown into folds and hummocks against the stable ground downslope. Sliding, without rotational movement, is also common, but slides do not have the regular form of slumps and they pass imperceptibly into flows of various kinds as the water content of the soil increases.

Landslips, like gullies, occur even in terrain unaffected by man and on slopes well protected by dense vegetation, but they are less frequent and less extensive and they quickly become grown over by colonizing vegetation. Under a grazing and burning regime in deforested country they remain and extend as permanent features of the landscape, contributing to the sediment load of the streams and reducing the economic value of the land.

'*Bunker*' *erosion*. This is common throughout the country on all moderate to steep slopes, especially where soils and subsoils are loose and friable. The crescent-shaped bunkers are caused by sheep lying and rubbing against a bank or steep slope until a little bare shelf has been formed. The process is often started by rabbit burrowing. Bunkers are often associated with a general weakening of the vegetation and the occurrence of sheet wash; they may become confluent and the whole slope reduced to bare soil or rubble (plates 12 and 13). Quite gentle peat slopes may be badly damaged in the same way and some of the best examples of this may be seen in the Sperrin Mountains of Northern Ireland.

River bank erosion. Loss of land by river bank erosion and the inundation of riverside flats is symptomatic of bad catchment management. The undercutting of river banks is associated with the formation of a wide flood channel across which minor divisions of the normal river flow meander. The land lost to the river may be reasonably good arable or grazing land, in which case moderately expensive protection measures are justified, or it may be rough grazing of low value. Even the land of low value is generally of better quality than the surrounding hill slopes, especially if it forms part of an alluvial plain. Apart from bank slumping, debris slides on the faces of old river terraces are frequently caused by undercutting in this way and good examples can be seen on both banks of the River Nethy above Nethy Bridge.

Wind erosion. Erosion by wind is a natural phenomenon along the coastal strip, where the severity of exposure is comparable with that of the mountain tops. This erosion is frequently extended by overgrazing of the sandy grass swards (machair) developed behind the fixed dunes and by trampling of the dunes themselves (plate 13). Injudicious ploughing of the level machair has also led at times to disastrous blowing of the sandy soil. Where the machair has a basis of shell sand it is particularly important in the local agricultural economy since the hinterland is generally an acid blanket bog of low grazing value. Many sea sands, apart from true shell sands, contain some intermixture of shell fragments, *foraminifera*, or algal limestone so that the turf that develops initially is relatively nutritious compared with the vegetation of moorland and bog.

In the absence of effective grazing control these swards, like the better hill grasslands, are heavily punished by domestic stock and the turf so weakened by grazing and trampling that the sand is exposed and begins to blow. The machair lands have taken an immensely long time to develop from the accumulation of blown sea sand, and they represent an important local resource which is too often squandered by unremitting exploitation. The soils are humus-deficient and depend for their stability on the surface mat of grass roots.

It will generally be found that conservation measures on the machair are taken only when damage has become extreme and that these measures take the form of sand-catching obstructions, pegging, thatching, and so on, while the overgrazing continues as before wherever there is anything left to graze.

Deep Peat Erosion

Much discussion has taken place in the past about the extent to which erosion of deep peat deposits (plate 9) is natural or a man-made phenomenon resulting from burning and grazing. Advocates of natural origin advance two main processes by which active bog growth could be replaced by recession and erosion:

(1) Upward growth of the bog eventually cuts off plant roots from contact with the mineral substratum and so reduces the quantity of nutrients in the recycling system. The vegetation is then dependent on mineral additions from the atmosphere to replace those lost by leaching and in the dead plant material going to form the peat.

(2) Climatic change in the direction of either wetness or dryness, or of increasing fluctuations in the evapotranspiration regime, leads to retrogressive changes in the vegetation and erosion of bog.

Advocates of the second theory advance the arguments that are considered in the section on moor burning (p. 37). Our own observations of peat-forming vegetation indicate that, once vegetation has been destroyed and deep peat laid bare, the surface is recolonized only in fairly exceptional circumstances; the normal situation is one in which growth of new vegetation is either exceedingly slow or else the extent of bare peat continues to increase without further interference. This situation is inherent in the physical and chemical composition of peat and must always have been so since the first deep, blanket peat began to form. The greater the altitude the more exceptional does re-growth appear to be. However, only direct mechanical disturbance and fire appear to be capable of destroying peat-forming vegetation to an extent which leads to erosion on the familiar scale. Mechanical disturbance can include bog bursts, the formation of sub-surface drainage channels leading to collapse of the surface, and numerous small scale phenomena related to these. Fire, which completely kills surface vegetation or destroys the upper layers of the peat itself, is more important than disturbance.

Mineral impoverishment of the bog surface, increased wetness, or desiccation certainly lead to vegetation changes but these changes take place slowly, and there are always some species available to maintain a complete surface cover even if these are only mosses and lichens.

If these observations can be generalized it is clear that there would be a considerable extent of eroding peat today, even in the absence of man, as the accumulated result of centuries of minor mechanical effects and, more important, natural fires. There is ample evidence of natural forest fires antedating the appearance of man upon the scene and of these fires extending to the shrubby moorland vegetation above the forest limit. The erosion of high level bogs could have started in this way.

It is also clear that the greater incidence of fires and direct mechanical interference with bog surfaces consequent upon man's activities would increase the rate at which bare peat surfaces were formed and exposed to disturbance by frost, wind, and rain. Fire, if severe, need extend only once to the upper limit of deep peat formation to initiate continuing erosion. The erosion of high level bogs cannot be used, therefore, as evidence for or against the naturalness of deep peat erosion. Some badly dissected areas at high level will have been initiated by natural fires, others by man-made fires; it is impossible to distinguish the cause in any particular instance nor is it of great importance now.

Among the situations where recolonization of the bared peat can take place the most important are: (*a*) formation of hollows by local smouldering of the peat followed by pool formation, *Sphagnum* recolonization, and the appearance of higher plants in the course of the local succession; (*b*) formation of redistributed peat flats of high water content but not subject to permanent flooding, followed by the appearance of *Eriophorum angustifolium*, one of the few species able to colonize and stabilize such a surface. Normally, the peat surface laid bare by confluent hagging is subjected to disturbance by wind and rain and is stirred up by frost movement for at least six months of the year, so that it is too unstable to allow plant colonization. The level of mineral nutrients in any particular peat is also an important factor in colonization once some stability has been assured.

Wet oxidation of peat is also a possibility in certain circumstances where micro-organisms capable of causing this are able to grow. It may be an important factor in maintaining bare patches and channels in inactive or eroding low level bogs.

Vegetation which breaks down under repeated burning to permit peat erosion includes deer hair sedge–heather moor, cotton grass–heather bog, cotton grass–crowberry bog and blaeberry–heather moor. Pure heather moor, on the other hand, regenerates to some extent within one year of the normal fire and, even where some of the surface peat has been consumed, its tough fibrous composition provides a suitable, stable substratum for colonization by heather, etc.

Notes on Specific Erosion Sites

Although the signs of land misuse are universal throughout the Scottish uplands twelve sites, mostly visible or easily accessible from the main roads, have been chosen by way of illustration. These are not necessarily the most glaring examples of particular features but are reasonably representative.

Slochd Mor, Inverness-shire (plate 7). This rocky cutting borders the A9 road and the Perth to Inverness railway line between the villages of Carrbridge and Tomatin. The original vegetation here was almost certainly pine–juniper forest but the cleft itself probably carried a patch of mixed broad-leaved trees on acid brown soil under the influence of water percolation from the bedrock. Burning and grazing at some time in the past seem to have led to the development of a good bent–fescue turf on the brown soil and heather moor with juniper scrub on the mor humus of the surrounding slopes. Today, scree formation is taking place rapidly on the heather slopes, the grass turf is fragmented and the brown soil mostly gone. Few junipers remain and even the heather has been killed out in patches through repeated burning and continuous sheep grazing. Here was a local patch of enhanced fertility and shelter that should have been conserved from both economic and aesthetic points of view; it is doubtful if the full rehabilitation treatment of fencing and protection from fire could save much from the wreck now. (Map reference: NH 840252)

Creag Dubh ridge, Inchriach, Inverness-shire. In April 1959 a moor fire spread out of control to burn a substantial area of this ridge above 2,000 ft (600 m) between Creag Dubh and Clach Choutsaich. The vegetation that it was intended to burn consisted of deer hair sedge and heather, with some patches of cotton grass and heather, but the fire ran uphill onto dwarf crowberry–heather mat, some of it rich in reindeer lichens, and was stopped only by the crest of the ridge. Patches of thin peat burned along with the shrubs and the fire was followed by some surface wash of the bared peat and sandy gravel. Plant recolonization has hardly begun yet, and it is doubtful if the original vegetation will ever return. (NH 902040)

Carn Eilrig, Rothiemurchus, Inverness-shire. The west slopes of Carn Eilrig have been too severely burned above 2,000 ft (600 m). The vegetation here consisted of deer hair sedge and heather on a particularly free-draining site. Sheet wash of the surface peat and mineral soil horizon is taking place, and incipient scree formation can be seen in many places. (NH 935054)

Roadside west of A9 between Newtonmore and Kingussie, Inverness-shire (plate 12). This area is trivial in extent but important in that it shows so clearly what is taking place on a larger scale in places not so obvious to the passer-by. A small patch of felled woodland has been heavily grazed by sheep. Sheet erosion and the formation of bunkers in the steep slopes are well advanced, exposure of the tree roots providing some measure of the soil already lost. (NH 744003)

Moorland south of Daviot Station, Inverness-shire. This is the site of a moor fire started from the railway in the summer of 1955. Areas of thin, dry peat which burned into the mineral soil are still covered by a pure carpet of *Polytrichum* moss with patches of the tiny annual grass *Aira praecox*. The moss occurs mainly in patches of a few square yards but there are larger areas of several acres. Heather has recovered well on most of the burned ground, although there is still an abnormal proportion of *Erica cinerea*. There has been surprisingly little peat or mineral soil erosion although some sheet wash and gullying can be found. Birch and willow seedlings are widespread wherever peat cover has been burned away, and the further course of succession depends on how quickly rotational burning is introduced once again. In the absence of fire the moor could develop into a mosaic of birch– willow scrub and long, mossy heather; rotational burning will bring about extension of the *Polytrichum* patches and perhaps renewed erosion. (NH 747382)

Drumochter Pass, Perthshire–Inverness-shire. The steep, heathery slopes flanking the A9, principally on An Torc and Creagan Doire Dhonaich, show increasing gullying and scree formation, largely as a result of heather burning. The underlying slope deposits are loose and once the protective capping of peat and heather has been destroyed they are easily excavated by run off from above during heavy rain. (NN 623764)

Glen Tilt, Perthshire (plate 8). The steep, grassy slopes below Creag Mhor and opposite Forest Lodge have been deeply gullied in places due, at least in part, to the weakening of the turf by grazing. The natural vegetation of these slopes is probably mixed deciduous woodland, but a properly managed grass sward should be quite adequate to prevent erosion. The treatment of the slopes above the gullied grassland is probably equally to blame and has resulted in flashy run off during storms. (NN 934742)

Inchnadamph, Sutherland. The steep slopes on the north side of the Traligill Burn have suffered considerably from sheet erosion of the limestone soil due to overgrazing by sheep. Limestone bedrock and rubble are now exposed in many places and the eroding, reddish soil is conspicuous. A fertile soil such as this should not be visible at any time of the year in the equable climate of the north-west Highlands, and the continuing erosion is particularly incongruous in a National Nature Reserve. The slopes on the south side of the burn show gullying due to undermining by water and the collapse of the tunnel roof. This is a common form of erosion in other parts of the world where run off from slopes of exposed bedrock meets the valley till or where rocks are highly calcareous. The Inchnadamph area also shows many fine examples of peat erosion brought about by frequent burning of cotton grass–heather bog and deer hair sedge–heather bog. (NC 280210)

Duntulm and Storr Rocks, Isle of Skye. Both these areas show sheet erosion, gullying, and slipping of steep, basalt soil slopes due to continuous grazing and movement of sheep. The damage can be matched in any of the Tertiary basalt areas of the west Highlands. (NG 410734)

West slopes of Fionchra, Isle of Rum. The west side of this hill is cut by a number of short gullies, one of which is impressively deep. These gullies are of the usual form, beginning where the grass turf on colluvium and glacial debris meets the bedrock above, and discharging onto level, marshy ground by way of a steep debris cone. It will be interesting to see if stabilization begins now that sheep have been removed from the island, but it is probable that no appreciable change will be observed until deer are excluded from the immediate vicinity and some regrading, pegging and thatching are carried out. (NG 330005)

South end of Achnashellach Forest on the east side of Glen Carron, Ross-shire (plate 11). Outside the forest fence the slope exhibits sheet erosion of peaty soil towards the crest of the ridge, with gullying of the mineral soil lower down the slope. The contrast with complete tree and heather cover and absence of erosion within the forest fence is striking. The lower part of the eroding slope has recently been fenced and planted, apparently with the idea of checking the upward extension of the gullies, but nothing seems to have been done with the upper slopes where the trouble starts. Difficulty may be experienced in maintaining the upper fence across active gully extensions. (NH 012480) *Cairngorm, Inverness-shire* (plate 14). The erosive agent at this site is one which will probably become increasingly important as the Highlands are developed as the nation's playground—the mechanical impact of too many people on a small area. Road building and other construction works have also left large areas of denuded and unsightly peat and stony debris. Looking up to Cairngorm from Aviemore one can observe first of all the diagonal scar of the access road, the naked patches around the White Lady Shieling and the anastomosing system of tracks associated with the snow fields of Coire Cas. A local cloudburst, to which the Cairngorms seem particularly liable, centred upon the corrie could now cause catastrophic gullying and perhaps endanger the buildings and chair lifts. (NH 995050)

At close quarters it is clear that the dwarf shrub and moss mat of the higher slopes of Cairngorm are taking heavy punishment from tracked vehicles and tractors, human feet, and the clipping action of skis over shallow snow and *verglas*. The proportion of bare raw humus and scree is increasing alarmingly throughout the summit area. If skiing development is extended to other corries it is to be hoped that some thought will be given to minimizing the disturbance of soil and vegetation in these sites where revegetation is extremely difficult to effect. These problems are not mentioned in the Cairngorm Area Report (1967) although students from Aberdeen University are now studying them.

3. Hill Farming

The hill sheep farmer is the principal user of Scottish hill land, whether alone or in conjunction with other enterprises such as cattle breeding and sport. Accordingly, a number of general topics will be discussed under the heading of hill farming. Many of these, for example, the bracken problem, are most appropriate here although others, such as moor burning, are common to other forms of land use.

Problems of Land Improvement

Considerable confusion is caused in ecological discussions and publications by the careless use of the terms 'overgrazing' and 'undergrazing'; agriculturists and ecologists frequently argue at cross purposes about them. The ecologist often refers to undesirable changes in vegetation and habitat brought about by a combination of burning and/or overgrazing, while the same area is manifestly undergrazed from the farming point of view. The ecologist should qualify the term overgrazing when he means only that natural succession has been arrested and that tree and shrub seedlings are being destroyed by wild or domestic animals. It is, however, legitimate for him to speak of overgrazing when the vegetation is being weakened to such an extent that soil is being exposed and there is danger of accelerated erosion. The elimination of palatable species by selective grazing is overgrazing from the pastoral point of view, although the process may go unrecognized.

In one sense any vegetation which has to be burned to remain pastorally productive is being undergrazed. At the same time the weight of stocking between burns may be such that the few palatable species originally present, or attempting to colonize, are progressively eliminated, while undesirables such as *Nardus* and bracken are taking over.

Heather moor on the better mineral or shallow peat soils may be converted gradually to poor bent–fescue grassland by a system of burning and grazing. Where this is possible the stocking rate can be regarded as reasonable in spite of the fact that burning forms part of the management. Inspection of the grass sward so formed will reveal whether local overgrazing is taking place or not. On deeper peats the same frequency of burning and density of stocking might be disastrous although the original plant communities appeared superficially alike. Whether it is desirable to convert all the heather moor that can be so converted to grassland depends on other factors such as the ratio of heather to grassland on the hirsel.

Even where burning does not complicate the picture it is desirable to qualify the terms 'overgrazing' and 'undergrazing' in some way, usually with reference to particular species or to the season of the year. In general terms, most of the vegetation of the uplands is undergrazed in the period June to August, with the exception of small areas of grassland and marsh on lime-rich soils in otherwise peaty districts. In the winter and spring months overgrazing extends from the lime-rich patches to a wide range of vegetation including, very often, small areas of young heather and poor bent–fescue grassland. The bent–fescue grasslands are often deceptively green when overgrazed, owing to a thick mat of feather mosses filling the spaces between the grasses which would show up as bare soil in a dry climate (plates 2 and 4).

MOOR BURNING

Systematic moor burning is scarcely two centuries old, but it is the direct descendant of the deliberate forest and scrub fires which are primarily responsible for the emergence of the Scottish uplands as moorland rather than forest habitat. Natural forest fires have left their traces in the peat, even as far back as the Atlantic Period when the climate is supposed to have been even damper than it is today. There is some evidence that these fires did not stop at the altitudinal limit of the forest but spread upward through the sub-alpine scrub to the dwarf-shrub heaths of the low-alpine zone. The low-alpine heaths were probably dominated by heather below 3,000 ft (900 m), as they are today in the eastern Highlands, and they would have burned readily. Bog surfaces too must have been burned in really dry weather.

The structure of these early forests is unknown, but it was almost certainly different from that of the native oak, birch, and pine wood-lands that survive today. In some places the transition from forest to moorland as a result of fire must have been early and rapid, in others delayed until the systematic burning of the eighteenth and nineteenth centuries. In the drier districts heather would gradually extend its hold over former forest ground until heather moorland stretched from sea level to the altitudinal limit of the species. In the wetter districts the land cleared of forest may have developed through a heather-domi-nated phase to a more sedgy vegetation, the persistence of the heather phase depending on the frequency of the fires.

This haphazard process, by which the grazing value of the original forest, scrub, and moorland was temporarily improved, developed into the present-day system of rotational burning for both sheep and grouse. In a relatively short time the practice has become so deeply ingrained as to be almost an article of faith, and any attempt at dispassionate reassessment is not well received.

Fundamentally, moor burning consists of removing the old, uneaten and uneatable plant growth to make way for the new, at the same time utilizing the old material as a light dressing of non-nitrogenous fertilizer. Obtaining the maximum benefit from burning, while keeping undesirable effects to a minimum, is a highly skilled business to which less attention is given today than formerly. General rules can be formulated but everything depends on the experience of the man on the spot, his appreciation of each locality and of the influence of the weather before and during the burn. This willingness to give the job really close attention is now rare and the average burn is a distinctly hit or miss affair which may or may not produce the desired effect, and which probably does a great deal of unnecessary harm. In any case, present-day economics of grouse moor and hill sheep farm management preclude the employment of the necessary staff to carry out moor burning in the way that past experience has shown it should be done (see p. 81).

Moor burning in the eastern half of the Highlands (approximately east of a line from Rannoch to Oykell Bridge) tends to perpetuate the heather moors that fire originally created, while in the wetter, western half of the region continued burning is tending to eliminate heather in favour of its competitors *Molinia*, deer hair sedge, cotton grass, and a few other species of minor importance. Young heather sprouts readily from the stool after burning and so produces a good ground cover fairly rapidly. Old and moribund plants are completely killed by the destruction of their foliage, and recolonization of the site has to be carried out by seedling heather. If the ground is damp and protected by a thick pad of mosses the chances of stool regeneration are good, but if the peat surface is dry and exposed the chance of a ground fire, with complete destruction of the heather roots, is increased. Kayll and Gimingham (1956) have shown experimentally that fewer stem bases regenerated after burning than after clipping, and that heather loses the ability to regenerate as it ages.

Much seedling regeneration after fire appears to arise from seeds already present in the surface peat so that too fierce a fire is not desirable, although moderate heating improves seed germination (Whittaker and Gimingham 1962). The bare patches which are generally found throughout the heather moor seem to be due to local smouldering of the peat surface with destruction of these seeds. By the time that seeds from an outside source reach the badly burned patches the peat surface has become toughened and lichen-encrusted, and unsuitable for heather colonization.

The arguments in favour of moor burning can be stated quite

briefly. For the manager of a grouse moor it produces a range of heather patches of all ages, young shoots for feeding and longer heather for nesting cover and protection from bad weather; that is, it enables a much larger population of grouse to exist than would be possible on a natural vegetation cover. For the hill sheep farmer it produces a succession of palatable young heather crops and herbaceous plant shoots richer in minerals through having absorbed them from the ashes of the fire. Following a spring burn, *Molinia* and other grass shoots may appear slightly earlier than they would otherwise have done, and they are more easily grazed by the animals. The enhanced mineral content of this herbage does not persist beyond the first season. The overall effect is once again the maintenance of a larger stock of animals than would be possible on the same vegetation in the absence of burning.

The grouse and sheep men deny that any price has to be paid or has been paid for this increased production, but ecologists and conservationists are not so confident of this, and some attempt has lately been made to construct a nutrient balance sheet for the moorland ecosystem. Losses from the system consist of leaching, volatilization during moor burning, wind and water erosion following a burn, and the removal of the animal crop. Accessions consist of the nutrients contained in rain water and air-borne dust, and nutrients released in the process of rock weathering.

The last quantity cannot be calculated, but it is probably unimportant where plant roots are confined to the peat layer. The other quantities have been estimated and it has been found that, with the possible exceptions of nitrogen and potassium, the loss of nutrients during and following a burn is insignificant in relation to the total quantities present in the soil–vegetation system and is exceeded by the input from rain over the period between fires. The removal of minerals in the animal crop is smaller still than either the normal level of soil leaching or the losses in moor burning (Allen 1964, Robertson and Davies 1965).

Previous studies had indicated a small but continuous decline of fertility under a moor burning regime, but it now seems as though current fertility decline, if present, must be regarded as insignificant. Questions left open by these investigations are the extent to which nutrient accessions in rain water are utilized by the plants before they pass beyond the reach of the roots in the drainage water, how the present level of fertility compares with that of the original ecosystem, and how that ecosystem might have been used in a less extravagant and destructive way. It is likely that the greater physical and chemical deterioration took place in the early stages of the conversion of mixed forest to moorland and monospecific forest.

Repeated moor burning reduces floristic variety, quickly to begin with but more slowly at each burning, and tends to produce either a pure heather crop or a stand of the poorest grasses and sedges as indicated above. In much the same way the forest fires of the past, if they did not actually result in moorland, were probably instrumental in forming the pure stands of birch and pine whose remnants persist today.

With the reduction of floristic variety goes an impoverishment of the dependent animal life with the increased risk of violent fluctuations in animal numbers. The well-known plagues of heather beetle and antler moth are examples of this. Heather beetle plagues are associated not with the presence of old heather in urgent need of burning, as the exponents of regular burning claim, but with the presence of dominant, uniformly aged heather at any stage. Damage to older heather by the beetle may be more obvious and more liable to result in the death of the plants.

Tree and shrub seedlings are destroyed more effectively by burning than by animal browsing. Where small areas grazed by sheep, but not subject to burning, can be watched for a number of years it will be found that the presence of the animals does not prevent the gradual return of scrub and woodland to rough heather ground, provided that the animals do not concentrate upon the area for shelter or some other reason, and provided tree and shrub seeds are available to initiate colonization.

One of the most important effects of fire is its selective action in favouring shallow-rooted species, which are unable to obtain from the lower soil horizons mineral nutrients released by the weathering of the parent rock or leached from the surface by percolating rain water. Trees and tall shrubs, being deeper rooted, can do this to some extent and partially counteract the process of podzolization. Hence the species encouraged by fire are those that form raw humus, while the most easily eliminated species are those that form a milder, more biologically active humus. The mild humus plants are generally more palatable to animals.

Besides the encouragement of bracken, deer hair sedge, *Nardus*, *Molinia*, and *Juncus squarrosus* by burning, other undesirable changes in the abundance of certain species can be observed. The last juniper thickets, relics from the days of the pine forests, are also being steadily eliminated in the eastern Highlands; they have already disappeared from the west Highlands except on the smaller islands in lochs. Pigott (1964) has shown that the common nettle is an indicator of high soil fertility and that it is particularly dependent on large supplies of available phosphorus. McVean and Ratcliffe (1962) have described the growth of nettle clumps in the relict juniper thickets mentioned above and published figures showing large quantities of available phosphorus in the soil below dwarf juniper mats. These facts indicate how senseless is the present continued destruction of living juniper and juniper humus by fire. In Norway the grazings above the forest limit are sometimes improved by grubbing out the juniper bushes, a system which retains both litter and humus for utilization by forage plants while maintaining the stock of juniper in the surroundings.

The surface of the peat in areas subjected to repeated burning takes on a rubbery or greasy skin, which affects water penetration and aeration. This is due partly to physical changes in the peat and partly to the growth of algae and lichens on the surface. Laboratory tests, in which it has been shown that burning brings about an increase in the permeability of peat to water, have been carried out on small samples already consolidated by years of burning and have not followed the long-term effects of exposure of the burned surface to weathering. Rennie (1962) has shown how lacking in aeration moorland humus may become in comparison with the forest humus from which it has sometimes been derived and how quickly a substantial improvement takes place following the growth of either coniferous or broad-leaved trees upon the condensed peat.

One of the great difficulties in applying a long-term experimental programme of soil fertility investigation to the moor burning problem is the absence of control areas carrying the original soil and vegetation complex which could be used as yardsticks. Fragments of surviving native woodland could be felled and converted into rotationally burned moorland in order to investigate the changes taking place, but even this would not be entirely satisfactory since the surviving woodlands are not fair samples of the original forest cover.

There are other difficulties in finding a satisfactory expression of fertility common to all analytical work with peat samples. There is first of all the considerable volume–weight distortion which renders impossible a straight comparison of results from peats and mineral soils, and there is the difficulty of deciding what proportion of the nutrients present in humified and partly humified plant material are immediately available for new growth. Biological assay of the samples would probably be the most meaningful method of comparison and, in a sense, this is already available from the results of attempts at afforestation on different moorland sites (p. 60). Eggeling (1964) has also pointed out that grouse can be regarded as a test animal and that the decline in grouse numbers can be regarded as some indication of the extent of habitat deterioration which has taken place over the last century or so (see also p. 79).

Another possible approach to the problem would be an attempt at reconstructing the original ecosystem. Unfortunately, the changes brought about by fire in a cool and wet climate appear to be irreversible for all practical purposes. The mere cessation of burning has little if any ameliorating effect, and the amount of effort which has to be expended by foresters in order to establish plantations on formerly forested uplands is a measure of the stability of the new complex.

From the restricted viewpoint of soil fertility, therefore, it would seem from the evidence advanced on p. 39 that the period of greatest deterioration is past and that continuation of the burning regime does little additional harm in many places. This may not be so in terms of local vegetation changes or where the acceleration of soil and peat erosion is concerned. As a general rule, applicable throughout the world, deterioration in soil fertility precedes the onset of active erosion, and removal of a biologically active (fertile) soil by wind and water is not common.

No matter how carefully burning is carried out accidents will happen and the fire become fiercer than intended or extend over too wide an area. This causes alarm only where buildings or plantations are threatened, but great damage can be caused to habitat and wildlife without raising general concern. Heathland above 2,000 ft (600 m) is often destroyed by uncontrolled fires. This heath is generally dominated by dwarf heather, but the rate of plant growth and the vulnerability of the habitat are quite different from those in the heather moor at low levels. In particular, the raw humus layer is thin and is easily destroyed, while the berry-bearing shrubs *Empetrum hermaphroditum* and *Arctostaphylos uva-ursi* may be killed. It is difficult to see that any of the usual benefits of burning accrue on such terrain while the harmful effects are many and obvious. The shrubs form a dense mat over the soil in a climate of considerable severity and when this mat has been burned irreparable erosion may result.

Where steep heather slopes are burned below rocky crags and cliffs the updraught is particularly fierce and in dry weather any tree and bush growth on the cliff ledges is destroyed. Through relative freedom from grazing and burning these ledges retain some semblance of the original forest and scrub vegetation. Pigott (1964) claims that the soil of the ledges is richer in available phosphorus than that of the surrounding burned country but this could well be an effect of the bird life that they attract. As well as small trees and bushes the ledges generally carry a greater variety of herbs, some species being virtually confined to these protected habitats in certain areas. Sheep often become crag-fast in attempting to reach the fresh grazing on the ledges, and this fact is used by the sheep farmer as an argument for burning the ledges with the rest of the hill. Ledge sites provide nesting cover for birds and harbourage for other animals in areas where cover of any kind is now at a premium.

The same remarks apply to all relict, unburned areas in native forest adjoining the moors or along stream gorges. Year by year the number of such oases is being steadily reduced, just as hedgerows and little fragments of rough ground and scrub are being eliminated from the lowland farming scene. Small islands in lochs often carry similar vegetation but these too are being reduced in numbers, inundation by hydroelectric schemes forming one of the latest hazards.

A great deal of moor burning is carried out without sanction after the legal date, especially in the remoter parts of the country. This is particularly apparent in years when a dry period of weather does not arrive until late April or early May; the temptation to burn then is considerable, when such fires can easily be 'accidental'. Late fires may destroy nesting birds as well as do damage to soil and vegetation greater than that from earlier fires.

Truly accidental moor fires are common throughout the year during periods of high evaporation, and these are particularly damaging during a summer drought when the peat itself has become dry enough to burn. The entire peat cover of an area may be destroyed by a summer fire such as that near Daviot, Inverness-shire in 1957 (p. 33).

An instructive zonation of vegetation can be seen along the railway in the neighbourhood of Slochd Summit on the Perth to Inverness line. The closer to the railway the more frequent the fires caused by sparks in the days of the steam locomotive. The innermost zone consists of loose peat dust with patches of willow herb, sorrel, thistles, and ragwort; next comes a belt in which mosses form a fairly complete carpet protecting the peat to some extent against erosion. Dominant *Erica cinerea* and *Erica tetralix* form the next zone, with mosses still abundant, and finally comes the region in which heather is able to recolonize the ground. The outer moss and *Erica* zones can be matched in many places where moor fires have been too fierce on a dry surface, or too frequent, or where pine, juniper and heather vegetation has been burned.

Frequently burned moorland and bog also suffers more severely from drought than less frequently burned land. This is partly due to lack of moisture retention by the rubbery peat; it is also due to the absence of a protective cover of bog mosses and plant litter which shield the ground surface from the direct rays of the sun and assist in the retention of a moist air layer next to the ground. It has been calculated that peat of this rubbery variety has only a narrow range of moisture content at which it is suitable for plant growth, and that rainfall of the order of only half an inch is sufficient to raise it from the point at which moisture is too strongly held to be available to plant roots, to the point at which moisture content is so high that it impedes plant growth through lack of aeration (Rennie 1957). This is not true of the friable, forest humus from which many moorland peats have been derived. Also, an untouched peat bog surface has a deep layer of moss and litter in which plant roots ramify at a moisture and air content more favourable to them than that of the underlying peat. This layer is destroyed or reduced by burning so that plant roots are confined to the dense peat layers and subject to alternating moisture lack and oxygen deficiency. In longer periods of dry weather, heather and other species may even be killed outright where shallow peat overlies impervious glacial drift or bedrock on south-facing slopes.

THE BRACKEN PROBLEM

Bracken is a highly successful and aggressive species and it is widely distributed in both temperate and tropical regions throughout the world. It has probably been increasing its range in this country ever since the start of wholesale deforestation, because it is kept in a subordinate position by tree cover although able to persist in all but the densest forest. Several factors probably combined to keep its advance within bounds until recent times. One of these was the formerly higher human population in upland districts; the people put bracken to many uses and grazed substantial numbers of cattle on the high ground in summer. It is also probable that successions of severe winters and late spring frosts formerly destroyed both underground stems and young fronds so that the rate of spread was limited. The present-day ratio of sheep to cattle, and repeated moor burning are favourable to the spread of bracken, owing to the harmful effects that these have on its main competitors such as all trees and shrubs, heather and the better grasses (plate 15).

Whatever the reason for the bracken advance it is certainly firmly established today and not even the latest selective herbicides seem likely to oust it from its strongholds. Bracken likes a warm or mild, moist climate with shelter from frosts and strong winds, a fertile soil and free drainage. Where it finds these in the absence of both cultivation and a dense forest shade it forms a complete ground cover up to six feet or more in height and excludes practically all other plants. The thick winter mat of dead fronds excludes competitors that might utilize the bracken's dormant period just as effectively as the tall stand of summer foliage does. An area dominated by bracken is useless for grazing and frequently expensive to afforest on account of the repeated weeding required in the first few years of the young plantation.

44

Ploughing is the most effective treatment for bracken infested ground and no further trouble will be experienced if the area can be kept under rotational cropping or improved pasture. When seeded to pasture constant vigilance is required to prevent re-invasion of the grass sward from the margins. Broken and rocky ground which cannot be brought under the plough is generally difficult to treat by systematic bracken cutting also. Even cutting with scythe or sickle will leave little patches of fronds round rocks or scrub from which re-invasion takes place. Complete control demands regular cutting at the right time of year combined with pasture improvement and adequate grazing.

If the bracken infested ground cannot be ploughed nor kept cut conversion to forest is the only way of rendering it productive. If the ground is so broken that a regular tree canopy cannot be established then the bracken will survive afforestation, but it will be a subordinate species and play a role approximating to its natural one.

The total number of species in a dense bracken stand is small but, at least, it can be said that under it no further site deterioration takes place. In fact, bracken has the reputation of being a moderately phosphorus-demanding species and, through its thick frond litter and rhizome mat, of accumulating a certain amount of phosphorus in the surface soil. Under its dense cover of living and dead fronds the soil is also safe from erosion, so that a period under bracken may eventually benefit a soil threatened by over-exploitation. The fertility trends under a bracken 'climax' on soils of low nutrient status require investigation.

Nicholson (1964) has recently made the point that past bracken utilization may have militated against its complete control since it would have been advantageous to conserve the stocks of so useful a plant. He also warns that the indiscriminate destruction of bracken by modern methods could open up formerly protected areas to uncontrolled grazing and thus dissipate a potential fertility resource.

Bracken will not invade wet peat and hence it is prevented from colonizing deer hair sedge and cotton grass moor, much *Molinia*–heather moor and pure *Molinia* grassland. Raw humus, if well drained, is no deterrent so that bracken is a common constituent of blaeberry–heather moor, pure blaeberry and heather communities, and peaty grasslands; indeed it may invade these and take over as it does on mineral soils. In its invasion of the drier, peaty sites it is greatly assisted by fire which sweeps through dwarf shrub vegetation at a time when the bracken is still dormant. It then emerges to benefit from the temporary absence of competitors and the top dressing of plant ash. A newly burned peat surface is also ideal for the germination of bracken spores and growth of the prothallus if it is kept constantly moist—as it generally is during a normal summer. In this way burning encourages the formation of fresh centres of bracken infestation as well as spread from established colonies (plate 15).

To sum up, bracken is a problem mainly to the less intensive land user, particularly to the unprogressive pastoralist; under a regime of ecologically determined land use most of the difficulties would disappear. If a cheap and efficient herbicide capable of destroying bracken is eventually developed it could bring in its train more problems than it solves, even if suitably selective in action. At the moment too many land users are apparently content merely to grumble at bracken while waiting for some spectacular form of chemical control rather than getting on with the job of eradication using the slower but quite effective methods already available.

PEAT UTILIZATION

It has been estimated that the total workable peat in Scotland amounts to 600 million tons (6,096 million kg) of peat solids, representing a peat cover over 1,700,000 acres (687,990 ha) at an average depth of 2 ft (60 cm). One million acres of these peat lands are also capable of improvement and use for agriculture or forestry (Scottish Peat 1962). The general conclusion of the second report of the Scottish Peat Committee was that development of peat resources for fuel on a large scale would not be advisable under existing economic conditions but that development was technically feasible and might be desirable at a future date. Forestry and agriculture will therefore remain the principal uses of peat land for some time, and there need be no fear of undesirable changes resulting from wholesale removal of the peat cover.

It is tempting to regard deep peat deposits as regulators of local run off in view of their sponge-like characteristics, but their capacity as water storage bodies has never been established and it has yet to be demonstrated that they prolong stream flow significantly in time of drought. After a period of dry weather an untouched bog surface probably will act as a regulator of run off, particularly if rainfall is heavy and prolonged, but the number of occasions on which this is useful in ameliorating floods is probably small. Nevertheless, it remains true that an intact bog surface is more desirable hydrologically than an eroding one. A joint hydrological investigation is at present being carried out by the Hill Farm Research Organization and the Macaulay Institute for Soil Research on a 17 acre (7 ha) peat bog catchment on Blacklaw Moss, Lanarkshire.

On accessible lowland bog, with underlying soil of good potential fertility, a system of surface cultivation, followed by removal of the loose material for later incorporation in the skinned land and the utilization of the uncovered peat for fuel, has been devised. There are few areas left in Scotland where workable lowland peat lies upon potentially fertile soil.

The same system might be used where the underlying soil is of poor potential, but the economics of the process would be less favourable. The economics of bog surface cultivation for arable cropping by itself, without peat utilization, have yet to be ascertained in Britain although a great deal of progress has been made in Eire.

The development of peat land as improved pasture and as forest plantation is dealt with in other chapters (pp. 48, 49, and 60).

HILL LAND IMPROVEMENT

The Natural Resources (Technical) Committee (1957) estimated that 750,000 acres (303,525 ha) of rough grazing in Scotland were capable of improvement.

Three tools are available for raising the fertility and productivity of hill land by improving the botanical composition of the pasture and enabling a heavier stocking of sheep and cattle to be maintained. These are grazing control, fertilization, and reseeding. Their correct manipulation forms an interesting exercise in applied ecology.

Hunter (1964) has shown how fencing alone can be employed for a more effective use of existing fodder resources. This depends on the recognition of two fundamental classes of hill grazings, the mull swards which consist of all varieties of bent–fescue communities, with or without bracken infestation and intermixture with *Nardus*, sweet vernal grass and heath grass, and the mor swards which include *Nardus*, *Molinia* and *Calluna* dominated communities.

By dividing the majority of the mull types from the majority of the mor types greater control of grazing can be maintained relatively simply, and a better balance in the utilization of winter and summer fodder obtained. The bent–fescue swards tend to be grazed heavily at all times of year except when completely bare in winter and early spring so that they are constantly maintained at less than their potential productivity. The remaining pastures are utilized to any extent only in winter and early spring when little else is available, so that a summer surplus of the mor types is normal. If hill cattle are to be introduced as a means of controlling the coarser vegetation of the mor and gley soils and boosting productivity, then fencing of some sort is essential, otherwise there will be an even greater shortage of winter keep and competition for the better mull grazing will reduce the sheep stocking.

Pasture improvements without fencing may upset the balance of hill grazing and lead to problems of management such as a sudden or increased necessity for winter feeding. In any case, a decision as to whether winter feeding is to form a part of the system must be made before deciding on the form of improvement to be undertaken. For each type of hill ground there is a ratio of bent–fescue sward to other types which is optimal in the sense that neither summer over-production of the one nor winter scarcity of the other is experienced. Mull grazing at 15 per cent of the total area is generally the critical ratio above which it is difficult to obtain a stocking increase as a result of fertilization and reseeding. Above this level the introduction of cattle in summer, together with fertilization of the existing vegetation, may be sounder policy than the reseeding of selected areas.

Ground limestone and rock phosphate or basic slag are the usual fertilizers applied to hill ground, since calcium and phosphorus are the mineral nutrients most generally deficient there. Nitrogenous manures are not applied since even the best of hill pastures cannot give an adequate return for such an expense, and it is wiser to rely upon the stimulating effect of lime and phosphate on nitrogen fixation by the existing white clover. The fertilizer application may be accompanied by discing or harrowing to break up the moss mat and improve soil aeration.

Reseeding with better grasses and clover may be carried out as part of the improvement scheme but it is generally more satisfactory to do this after ploughing under the old sward and following up with a complete fertilizer. Only the better areas of bent–fescue sward will repay the cost of this operation, and fencing is again essential if the full benefit of the treatment is to be obtained. The improved pasture can then be used as complementary to the larger areas of rough grazing, allowing the animals a limited time upon the improved section before returning them to the unimproved hill. With careful management a gradual extension of the enhanced fertility can be obtained in this way.

Certain types of blanket peat land will respond to seeding and fertilization without ground treatment. This method has become known as bog or moorland 'regeneration', an expression which does not follow the long accepted ecological usage for part of the growth cycle of active *Sphagnum* bog. The treatment involves the use of the peat land as a mere physical medium for the growth of the better grasses and clover in the presence of added fertilizer. At the same time the native plants of the bog may respond strikingly to the application of the phosphate and become more palatable to the grazing animals. It is doubtful, however, if adding phosphate without reseeding would pay on even the most phosphorus-deficient peat since the capacity of the existing vegetation to respond to a higher level of mineral nutrition is inherently limited. While results on the deeper, wetter peats may be satisfactory to begin with they may prove unsatisfactory in the long run unless elaborate drainage work is undertaken. Shallow, colloidal peat overlying the less compacted forms of glacial till is the most successful subject for this type of reclamation. It is desirable to know something of local peat and bog vegetation before embarking on such a scheme.

Attempts at improvement by drainage alone are frequently made but it will usually be found that this has little effect on the botanical composition or growth rate of the vegetation. The moisture content of the peat remains unchanged away from the immediate vicinity of the drain. This is due to the strong water-retaining capacity of the peat. In general, all bog reclamation schemes have a greater chance of permanent success if carried out in a region of at least some periodic water deficit (see figure 1 and p. 15).

Another method of hill improvement, quite widely advocated at one time, which is now being re-investigated by staff of the Scottish Plant Breeding Station and the Nature Conservancy, is the use of irrigation water from streams and springs whose mineral content is rather higher than that of the water held in the surrounding, peaty slopes. This method is not universally applicable, but there are a number of locations where some improvement can be effected in this way at low cost. The addition of lime and phosphate to the poorer irrigation waters is also a possibility as a means of economical fertilizer distribution. Irrigation can also be used to kill off bracken infestation in bent–fescue sward, which will survive the waterlogging for a longer period than the fern.

LIVESTOCK

HILL SHEEP

Hill sheep farming as an industry is about 200 years old in the Highlands and considerably more in the Southern Uplands. The first sheep farmers moved north into Argyll around 1760 and into Caithness and Sutherland in the early years of the nineteenth century. By 1830 the revolution was complete and, except for some displacement by the rise of deer stalking in the nineteenth century, the position of sheep as the staple product of the uplands has remained unchallenged until recently.

The incomers had remarkably little difficulty in acclimatizing the imported sheep, which did well in the early years — probably because the incomers had the pick of the land which was previously understocked; also it had carried mainly cattle, which meant that the grazings would be in good heart for the change in use.

The earliest sheep farmers brought Blackfaced sheep. Cheviot sheep came later, after 1790 ,when Sir John Sinclair drew attention to the worth of the breed. The nineteenth century began with a boom in Cheviots on account of the demand for fine wool and this lasted until 1860 when the tide again turned in favour of the Blackfaces, mainly because of the increasing supplies of Merino wool imported from Australia and a consequent demand for coarser wool and a smaller carcase to suit the meat trade. The change was considerable; in 1860, 40-50 per cent of hill sheep were Cheviots, and by 1930, 12 per cent (Watson 1932). The position has not markedly changed in 1968.

An important development in the management of hill sheep was the introduction of Leicester rams in the late eighteenth century, for crossing with both Blackface and Cheviot breeds. Although the Leicester was not a hill breed the early maturing quality and size were an inducement to hill sheep farmers to use it. The cross proved ruinous to the hardiness of hill sheep. However, by 1850 it was common to cross Leicester rams with Blackface and Cheviot ewes to produce Greyfaced and half-bred animals for fattening and breeding on low ground, and the practice continues today. By 1870 whole flocks were sometimes crossed in this way. This necessitated the buying in of pure Blackface and Cheviot animals to maintain a pure flock.

From 1850 onwards, many writers refer to a decline in the carrying capacity of upland grazings which seem to have been real. The reasons for the decline were various—the cessation of cultivation, loss of cattle and their replacement by the single, specialized mouth of the sheep, and the drain imposed on the land by a system of agriculture which involves the sale of stock with no replacement of minerals, especially phosphates and lime. Nevertheless, the effect took a long time to show. Watson (1932), quoting Macdonald, states that even in the oldest of the sheep farms a loss in carrying capacity did not show until 1880; in the next thirty years the carrying capacity of many Highland grazings dropped by 25 per cent.

Hill sheep farms are operated under circumstances in which livestock is the only product. The few crops that may be grown are required for feeding the stock in winter. The hill sheep farmer must make the best use he can of extensive rough grazing supplemented by minute areas of in-bye land which may be no more than two or three per cent of the total. Sheep and some cattle are the only agricultural answer, and both cater for the store market since these farms lack the home grown food necessary to carry the young stock beyond this stage economically.

Under rather better conditions with more in-bye land (say, more than one-fifth of the total acreage) more hay and tillage feed crops can be grown so that a wider range of animal products can be attempted.

The principal development then is the fattening of part of the annual lamb crop and the production of cross-bred lambs for sale to lowland farms. Usually the crosses are Blackfaced, Border Leicester ram to give a Greyfaced lamb or Cheviot, Border Leicester ram to give a half-bred lamb.

These livestock enterprises are based on the ewe flock and the breeding cattle beast and, in both instances, the number carried is restricted by the availability of winter food. The costs in running such farms tend to settle into a uniform framework and the main variation in returns arises on the output side. Returns are mainly determined by the size and nature of the lamb and calf crop and the prices at the time of sale. The farmer can try to control the first but he is helpless to influence the second except where, as in the case of the wool crop, prices are guaranteed by the government.

The main increase in the lamb crop can be achieved only by better feeding of the breeding stock, which increases the lambing percentage, the growth rates of lambs, and the incidence of twins under conditions when strong twins can be reared, and it reduces the proportion of barren ewes.

On hill sheep farms, better feeding is possible only within very restricted limits. In the smaller and more intensive stock-rearing farms it can usually only be achieved with the increased costs associated with more intensive cultivation and reclamation. It is not surprising, therefore, that both types of hill farm are heavily supported by government money. Duthie (1967) has reviewed the finances of 50 hill sheep and 40 stock-rearing farms in the east of Scotland. The hill sheep farms were on average 2,854 acres (1,142 ha) of which 2 per cent was arable; the average profit between 1961 and 1966 was £1,640, of which £1,506 was government subsidy. The stock-rearing farms were on average 754 acres (302 ha) of which 28 per cent was arable; over the same period, the average profit was £1,141 and the subsidy £1,416.

Thus, even with Government support, much hill farming is not paying its way. Chaffey (1967) states that hill farming employs one-tenth of those employed in agriculture and uses one-third of agricultural land in the broad sense. Yet, it contributes only one-thirtieth of the gross agricultural product. Government aid to hill farming is 40 per cent of the gross output compared with 20 per cent for agriculture as a whole. Moreover, lowland agriculture could quite easily replace all, or most of the present production from hill sheep farming.

One might reasonably ask why anyone persists with hill sheep farming. The answer is that some people have not, and sheep flocks have been withdrawn from a number of areas of the Central and West Highlands. But many sheep-men remain. Apart from the difficulty of changing to other jobs there is undoubtedly something about hill sheep farming which is attractive and which cannot be measured simply in terms of cash returns.

The reasons for the decline in hill sheep farming are thus part economic, part ecological. The ecological consequences of 200 years of ascendancy of sheep are considerable and have already been discussed.

HILL CATTLE

Hill cattle of the black Highland breed became an important factor in the rural economy of Scotland during the latter half of the eighteenth century (see p. 6). Various estimates have been made of the numbers exported annually from the Highlands and Haldane (1952) has calculated that the true figure could not have been far short of 60,000. Social and political changes resulted in the replacement of the cattle and human inhabitants by sheep and rendered it unlikely that there will ever be such a development of cattle breeding in the country again. However, the environmental factors are still virtually the same in spite of the reduction in forest and scrub cover and a probable reduction in both soil fertility and the abundance of palatable herbaceous species in the hill grazings.

Cattle are less selective grazers than sheep and the grazing habits of the two animals are largely complementary. Many areas of the Highlands are ideal for the reintroduction of hardy, free-ranging cattle. The post-war pioneering efforts at 'cattle ranching' were carried out on land of good average suitability and it is unfortunate that figures displaying the economics of the early schemes are not available. On the whole it seems wiser to consider further hill improvement schemes in terms of both cattle and sheep, since they obtain a certain amount of mutual benefit and the productivity of the hill grazings can be enhanced by this means.

Within recent years a few landowners have embarked upon rather ill-considered schemes on unsuitable land too steep, exposed, wet and infertile for the purpose. They have ignored the deleterious effect of cattle on hill drainage, have neglected fencing and omitted to carry out any local pasture improvement. The result has sometimes been quite devastating; colloidal peat has been laid bare and puddled while the better areas of bent–fescue sward have been so heavily punished that sheep already on the ground have suffered from lack of winter feed.

INTRODUCTION OF REINDEER

There is no doubt that reindeer once roamed the British Isles and there is even some indication that herds survived in the northern Highlands until Viking times.

An experimental reintroduction of reindeer from Sweden was begun at Glenmore in 1952 by the Reindeer Company Limited (or the Reindeer Council of Great Britain, as it was then). While it has certainly been demonstrated by this time that the species is capable of surviving and breeding to a limited extent in the Cairngorm area, the existence of competition for food supplies with the native red deer has not been disproved. It remains doubtful, therefore, if reindeer herding in the Highlands would be successful economically if undertaken on a larger scale, even although the reindeer is undoubtedly the more valuable animal.

Lichens, especially the tall, branching species of *Cladonia*, are the preferred winter food of the reindeer and, if the animals are to subsist on such a slow-growing plant, they require an extensive area of foraging ground. In the absence of adequate supplies of lichen the reindeer turn to other fodder and almost certainly seek out plants which are also sought after by the red deer. Lichen-rich and lichen-dominated vegetation, such as provides the optimum winter range for the reindeer, is severely localized in Scotland and, fortunately, the sites chosen for the reindeer introduction within the Glenmore National Forest Park did not contain any, otherwise an example of rare Scottish plant association would have been lost.

In summer the reindeer take a wide variety of grasses and other plants but the herbage is then so abundant that competition between the two species of deer should not arise. Once again it is winter fodder which is crucial, and if any attempt is made to proceed with plans for a wider introduction of reindeer in the Highlands more critical study of this aspect will have to be made.

The Hill Farming Research Organization

The HFRO became an independent grant-aided research organization in 1954, for the purpose of promoting research into hill farming problems. This was the culmination of ten years' work following the recommendations of the Balfour of Burleigh Committee in 1944.

The Organization has its own staff of scientists and operates three experimental hill farms, Glensaugh in Kincardineshire, Sourhope in the Cheviot Hills, and Lephinmore in Argyll. These localities provide contrasting situations for observation and experiment.

In 1954 two sections, animal and botanical, were set up, and in 1962 a third, agronomy, was added. But every effort was made to avoid rigid divisions between the scientific staff. Animal studies concentrated on the responses of sheep of varied breeding and at all stages of their life to the nutritional and climatic conditions prevailing under hill management systems. The aspects include growth and development, nutrition and climate, shelter, breeding, and health.

Botanical studies have followed various lines; first, there have been sociological studies of plant communities in an attempt to use vegetation as the principal indicator of environmental variation, second, the effects on vegetation of various management practices such as muirburn of heather and flying bent (*Molinia*), the grazing of heather, and the use of herbicides to control matt grass (*Nardus*) and bracken.

The agronomy section has investigated water in hill soils in relation to vegetation type and response as well as the more obvious practical matter of hill drainage.

Animal and plant studies were combined in an investigation into the grazing behaviour of sheep in relation to the mosaic of plant communities and also the relation of the intake of food to the consequent animal production (see p. 47).

Finally, there have been management studies—the up-grading of hill land and the wintering of hill ewes.

Much of this research is, of necessity, long-term. Its progress however, is described in periodic reports (HFRO 1954–8, 1958–61, 1961–4, 1964–7), and in published scientific papers listed at the end of each report.

There is a limit to what HFRO can do with present facilities. So far they have concentrated on the fundamental study of practical problems. They have rightly avoided a trial and error approach because this, while it may give a lucky answer, can never tell why this answer works, and therefore can never tell how good the answer is, or even if it is the whole answer; only research can do this.

Nevertheless, the HFRO are one-sided as a result of their remit. They must proceed as though hill farming were the main and best use of hill land. This precludes an appraisal of land use as a whole. However, this is a small proviso; their research is most valuable, especially that part that deals with the inter-relation of vegetation and grazing animal, and vegetation and fire.

4. Forestry

Scotland lacks a forestry tradition in the sense that there has never been a concerted attempt to conserve and manage the natural forest. On the other hand, Scottish foresters have a long and excellent record in afforestation, although the early forests were planned not for sustained yield but for amenity, or for a single timber crop. At the present day approximately $6\frac{1}{2}$ per cent of Scotland is forest covered, 80 per cent of this being privately owned.

Of the native forests remaining in Scotland only the pine stands are dignified by the name of forest and considered worthy of management. Birch, oak, alder and other unplanted woodland is generally classified as scrub and considered more of a hindrance than a help in reafforestation. The remaining native pine forests have survived for three main reasons: the low grazing value of the sites occupied, the abundant regeneration obtained until comparatively recently, and the value of the timber which made sporadic attempts at conservation worth while.

The oak has just managed to survive, largely because of its tendency to coppice after felling. Although oak is a valuable tree at maturity, regeneration is poor and growth slow so that it has seldom been considered worth while to exclude grazing animals entirely from the comparatively fertile sites that it occupies. Animals must be excluded for a number of years to obtain even coppice regeneration. The origin of surviving oak scrub should be borne in mind when evaluating the potential of a site since repeated coppicing leads to deterioration in the size and straightness of the stems.

Birch and alder woods have survived largely as a result of their prolific regeneration from seeds and their capacity to recover from fire and browsing damage (plate 18).

When an area containing fragments of native pine comes under forest management today some attempt is generally made to conserve the local strain, either by silvicultural treatment of the existing stands or by collection of seed stocks or shoot grafts before clear felling. Birch, oak, and alder scrub is cleared and burned, although a few of the better stems of *Betula verrucosa* may be retained temporarily. The practice of ring barking the larger hardwoods to save the expense of their removal has happily been abandoned.

MANAGEMENT OF NATIVE PINE FOREST

Management of an indigenous forest is generally influenced by the characteristics of the original forest on that site or, where this can no longer be ascertained, by the supposed characteristics of that forest. Jones (1945) has pointed out that, in apparently virgin forest, any type of structure may be encountered from even-aged, single story stands of the one species, to stands of intimately-mixed age of many different species and canopy heights. The mixed structure is rare, particularly in temperate regions where one may suppose that insufficient time has elapsed since the cessation of the glacial epoch for the development of truly climax forest. Fire and wind blow check the development of the more complex climax forms in temperate forest. The whole concept of the forest climax is now undergoing re-appraisal, and those who would now swing to the other extreme and discard it entirely are also suspicious of the 'natural forest system' as the ideal of silvicultural management.

For practical purposes the development of a straightforward method of maintaining soil fertility and a sustained yield forest is more important than striving to attain theoretical structures and regeneration systems that may or may not be successful.

Since regeneration of the desired species is the key to all management of natural or semi-natural forest the continued existence of self-sown pine forest in Scotland gives rise to anxiety on two main counts, one being the increasing numbers of wintering red deer in the un-fenced fragments of the native forest, the other the present composition of vegetation and surface humus, neither of which appear to be favourable to seedling establishment. The unfavourable features of the vegetation are: (*a*) dense *Sphagnum* under leggy heather and blae-berry in the open, western or high level forests; (*b*) felted and deep feather moss under dense blaeberry sward in the closed canopy eastern stands. It has long been known that heather is in some way particularly inimical to the development of the native pine seedlings as it is to the growth of planted exotic conifers. Recent indications have been obtained (Handley 1964) that this operates through the effect of mycostatic substances produced by the fungal partner of the heather roots on the mycorrhizal fungi of the tree roots so that dominant heather can exclude tree colonization from ground otherwise suitable.

The open woods with tall shrubs result from too sparse regeneration in the past, coupled with selective felling of the better trees; the dense woods with thick blaeberry follow upon mass regeneration and species impoverishment resulting from forest and heath fires. Both these situations stem from unwise land use and are not unrelated to the wider problem of general hill land deterioration.

Pine readily colonizes open, heathy areas wherever heather has recently been removed by fire, and it is known to have regenerated abundantly after forest felling and burning as lately as the eighteenth century when, it may be supposed, heather did not yet have such a stranglehold on the Highlands. The forests as they existed then would already have been more like those of today than the original Highland forests, which are thought to have lacked extreme segregation of species and age classes. Terrain that now carries pure pine probably grew mixed pine–birch forest with abundant alder, rowan, willow, aspen, bird cherry and juniper, with scattered oaks. Fires and occasional catastrophic wind throw there may well have been, and local thickets of even-aged pine and birch probably formed a proportion of the forest as a result. There must also have been extensive bog forests with poorly grown and scattered trees on deep wet peat.

Felling and burning both encourage mass regeneration but leave vegetation and surface humus less suitable for further regeneration unless fires again intervene. In particular, fire generally results in increased abundance and dominance of heather, which may occupy the ground before pine regeneration can take place. Repetition of this treatment in an oceanic climate already marginal for Scots pine has produced the regeneration difficulties of the present day, not suddenly since the eighteenth century as is sometimes implied, but as the end product of a long period of mismanagement. Even today small patches of mass pine regeneration can be found which recall some eighteenth century descriptions.

How then are the surviving woods to be preserved and if possible extended? There is scope for two lines of approach, one appropriate to commercial activity by private owners and by the Forestry Commission and the other appropriate to such organizations as the non-commercial Nature Conservancy. Steven and Carlisle (1959) have suggested the careful opening out of fully stocked stands of uniform age, with a final seeding felling arranged to coincide with a good seed year. Some controlled burning or destruction by selective herbicides of luxuriant heather in the immediate neighbourhood of seed-bearing trees would be beneficial, but sowing and planting would both be needed in less well-stocked areas and on such boggy patches as would repay the expense of adequate drainage.

A body such as the Nature Conservancy, on the other hand, could afford greater patience in waiting upon the long drawn out process of natural regeneration in many areas, while direct sowing could often be used as an alternative to planting on many peat and vegetation types. Conventional procedures could also be used for planting up gaps in open forest to increase general age diversity and for extending native forest onto the surrounding moorland wherever peat and vegetation are unsuitable for natural and assisted regeneration. The Nature

Conservancy would also be in a position to attempt the re-establishment of bog forest and more mixed stands of native species by both planting and seed sowing.

It is now generally agreed that locally collected seeds should be used in each forest and that a wide range of morphological types should be perpetuated in addition to those regarded as silviculturally desirable at the present juncture. The necessity for complete protection against deer is also recognized, although it must not be expected that fencing-alone will result in a good stand of young trees unless seedlings and saplings are already present. This point has often been missed in experimental fencing by private owners and public bodies alike, and surprise has been expressed that exclusion of deer from an area with adjacent seed trees has failed to result in regeneration. It must be emphasized again that all pine regeneration on a scale adequate to produce close canopy forest is confined to a period of several years following a moorland or forest fire. A good supply of seeds is also essential over this critical period, and if seedlings do not become established before the heather grows tall and the ground moss covered they will not do so unless fire again intervenes.

It may yet be found that the most convenient way of maintaining self-perpetuating native forest on small areas is by the encouragement of mixed stands whose dominants, pine, oak, alder, rowan, and birch, will depend upon the inherent fertility and drainage of the site, not by attempting to regenerate pure stands of these species.

PROBLEMS OF RE-AFFORESTATION

Problems connected with the replacement of forest cover upon the hill land of Scotland are of greater importance in the sphere of land use than the management problems discussed above. Although re-afforestation with exotic conifers did not begin with the establishment of the Forestry Commission in 1919, the appearance of large tracts of the uplands does have its origin at that important date. In Scotland the Forestry Commission now have a total holding of one and a quarter million acres although not all this land is planted or plantable.

The late Professor M. L. Anderson used to point out that the current rate of State planting saddled the present generation with a disproportionate and even unfair burden, and he proposed the term 'reparation' or 'restitution' planting for this wholesale and basically uneconomic restoration of forest unwisely destroyed by former generations. He claimed that such a programme could not be justified as a purely economic measure and that the creation of such enormous areas of even-aged forest was going to make it impossible to attain a system of sustained yield forestry.

The conflicting claims of forestry and hill sheep farming to considerable areas of our hill land forms one of the principal barriers to the development of a rational policy of land use. A start has been made to carry out joint land use surveys upon a restricted scale in the north of Scotland. This programme was begun in 1948 with a survey of the Oykell and Carron catchments in Sutherland, and three million acres (12 million ha) of the north of Scotland were surveyed over the next ten years. The method of approach, while not ideal, constituted an improvement over the former system of direct competition for each area of available land. The ground was first of all surveyed by acquisition officers of the Forestry Commission, who outlined all plantable ground. The maps thus prepared were submitted to the Department of Agriculture whose officers decided which plantable areas could be withdrawn from agriculture and allocated to the Commission whenever they came upon the market.

The Forestry Commission have normally obtained substantial acreages of hill land as a result of falling values in hill farming, and most of this land has, in fact, been more suitable for growing trees than for anything else. Some areas have been planted that could have been rendered more productive agriculturally had capital been available for their development, but examples of this kind have been magnified out of all proportion by the local farming community. It should be remembered that in the Strath Oykell scheme, for example, 8,000 acres (3,237 ha) have now been planted while sheep stocking has actually increased, and there are also some cattle on the hill where there were none before.

Local variation in soil and climate is such that the desirable integration of farming and forestry is not always easy to contrive, even where both enterprises are run under the one ownership, be it State or private. Young plantations must be protected against browsing animals and the cost of both stock and deer fencing is so high that small and awkwardly shaped areas of forest are seldom established. There is no doubt that shelter belts would be planted more often if fencing were unnecessary or cheaper to erect.

Moor burning also renders any integration of hill farming and forestry extremely difficult, for obvious reasons, and burning is a continual source of friction between neighbours and between departments of the same estate. The maximum difficulty is encountered where deer fencing and extensive fire precautions are both required in areas where sheep farming, deer management, and forestry co-exist.
Choice of species. If the choice of species were to be restricted to native British trees re-afforestation of the peaty uplands, while not perhaps impossible, would be a more difficult and less flexible operation. European larch and Norway spruce were brought into the country

during the late eighteenth century and other species from the Pacific coast of North America early in the nineteenth century.

The 'exotics' versus 'natives' controversy has now largely died down, but there are still diehards on both sides, the one group contending that the use of exotic conifers on the present scale is aesthetically and economically disastrous and the other dismissing as mere sentimentality any preoccupation with native species which have been placed in present possession of the country simply because of the accidents of plant distribution. While it is true that some features of plant distribution appear to be no more than accidents, and it is neither the climate nor other environmental factors operating within the British Isles that have denied us the larch or spruce as native species, it is also clear that dependence upon foreign species, still incompletely tested under British conditions, renders the future of home forestry less secure than it would otherwise be.

It is not sufficient that the initial growth of these introductions is satisfactory and mostly even superior to that of the few native species; initial success followed by retrogression and sometimes complete disappearance is a widespread feature of plant and animal invasions in the wild so that as long as forestry remains more than tree cropping on short rotations the danger of ultimate failure with some of the exotics remains.

With that said, however, we can accept the fact that foreign species from comparable climates and latitudes will be used here if they will grow well and there is a demand for their timber.

Forest establishment. Over the last few decades techniques of cultivation and fertilization have been evolved by the Forestry Commission Research Branch which result in the successful establishment of a number of coniferous species on formerly intransigent heathland and blanket bog. At first it seemed that this undoubted success completely solved the problem of re-afforestation on upland peat but it is now becoming apparent that other problems of tree nutrition, disease, and wind stability remain.

The standard method of establishment consists of ploughing at the required spacing of about five feet (1·5 m) followed by the planting of the young trees in notches cut from the side of the furrow slice, or in the bottom of the furrow, and the application of a few ounces of phosphatic fertilizer in their immediate vicinity. Lodgepole pine has proved to be the species giving most spectacular results with this method but Scots pine and the spruces have also been used under drier or more fertile conditions respectively.

Growth, especially of Lodgepole pine, has proved to be rapid for thirty years or so but in many places this has been followed by the onset of a growth check, the occasional appearance of mineral deficiency symptoms and sometimes widespread die-back of the young trees. Wind throw has sometimes occurred due partly to the alignment of the tree roots along drains where the water table is continually high. Die-back of European larch and Corsican pine have also caused some anxiety and outbreaks of spruce aphid have been spreading.

Growth check after the first thirty or forty years has also been experienced on the drier *Calluna* heaths of eastern regions, and Rennie (1953) has suggested that the release of nutrients from these heathland soils is too slow to sustain tree growth throughout the first rotation. If this is so, or even if the nutrient supplies are sufficient for the first but not subsequent rotations, then fertilization may be required for forest crops on the more impoverished soils, just as it has become normal practice for agricultural crops.

On deep peats phosphorus is often the mineral in shortest supply and once that deficiency has been corrected satisfactory growth is obtained for many years. At later stages deficiencies of nitrogen, potassium and other elements may appear as well as a recurrence of phosphorus deficiency. On the shallow, raw humus of heathlands nitrogen is generally the key element. Work is comparatively recent on these aspects of afforestation in which the removal of nutrients by the tree crop is balanced by fertilization and the natural accession of nutrients from soil weathering and in rainfall, and it is too soon to arrive at any general conclusion from it.

Besides the question of forest fertilization there has been a renewal of interest in the inclusion of soil-improving species with the main tree crop. Most tree species improve soil conditions on heath and moorland to some extent in that they bring about an amelioration of texture and drainage, increasing aeration and counteracting the downward movement of nutrients in the drainage water. Only the nitrogen fixers, such as the alders and leguminous trees, actually add to the total fund of nutrients. Workers in the United States have claimed an increase in the growth of the main tree crop where black locust (a legume) was included in the planting mixture. Alder is universally recognized as improving soil nitrogen status through the high nitrogen content of its leaf litter, but results from direct field experiments are not yet available from Great Britain.

Dimbleby (1962) has assembled evidence that the heathlands of north-eastern England, with their podzolic soils, have been produced by deforestation and burning from a former mixed forest cover on brown, mull humus soils. He claims that the return of birch cover to these heathlands results in the reconversion of the podzol to a brown forest soil, but this has been disputed. The available evidence suggests that birch can bring about considerable improvement of a soil in which the progress of deterioration has not gone too far but that it has little effect on seriously impoverished or badly degraded soils. It certainly seems to possess considerable powers of concentrating available nutrients on the surface, but if the nutrients are not present within the root zone, or if poor drainage renders them unavailable to the roots, there can be little effect.

As the forest canopies of plantations on peat become closed, the heath and moorland vegetation that occupied the ground is killed and replaced by a carpet of leaf litter with a sparse growth of woodland mosses and scattered vascular plants. After branch removal and thinning has resulted in an increase in light intensity beneath the canopy several different effects may be observed: the peat surface may be blown clear of litter in places and remain quite bare; there may be a light growth of woodland mosses and herbs such as *Holcus mollis* and *Oxalis acetosella*, or mosses, including species of *Sphagnum*, may become dominant.

In Northern Ireland Parker (1962) has described a form of secondary check in the growth of a spruce plantation, associated with the regrowth of dense *Sphagnum* moss on the woodland floor. He has also described some undesirable effects of fertilization on the underlying peat in other places leading to liquefaction and erosion of the surface. Clearly there are many aspects of tree growth on deep peat that require investigation and there is as yet no evidence supporting the claim of many foresters that, as their plantations age and are thinned, there will be a return to near natural structure and floristic composition of the forest vegetation.

State Forestry has put a great deal of capital into Sitka spruce which is an easy tree to establish and which has shown very good growth on fertile sites ever since it was first used for afforestation in Britain early this century. Even on poor sites it may grow well, at any rate in the early years. The Forestry Commission, faced after 1919 with a massive programme of re-afforestation, understandably found Sitka an asset, but in their enthusiasm have pushed the tree to the climatic and edaphic limit. As a result, its early promise is not likely to be realized over large areas of Scottish hill ground, particularly in the dry northeast. The crucial factor is the water balance of the tree, which is affected both by air humidity and ground water, and no part of Scotland quite duplicates the wet belt of the Pacific Coast of North America, the natural home of this species. Sitka grown on poor sites often cannot develop a root system adequate to maintain a sufficient water supply to the foliage. Under these circumstances attack by the spruce aphid (*Neomyzaphis abietina*) is severe and the tree is defoliated. In contrast, Sitka in its natural home does not suffer from aphid attack to anything like the same extent. Indeed, one view is that *Neomyzaphis* has become endemic in Britain because of the favourable environment for the pest produced by Sitka growing under poor conditions. Be that as it may, the situation is serious enough for the Forestry Commission to have devoted a large research effort to the problem. The reciprocal problem, that of the effect of Sitka on the site on which it grows, is largely unexplored although doubts have often been raised about the ecological good sense in the very widespread use of an exotic before fundamental tests on it have been made. Research on this problem is now in progress.

FUTURE DEVELOPMENTS

There is some argument at present about whether the maintenance of a large forest reserve is still a necessary part of the scheme for national defence, although it is certain that the main timber producers, Scandinavia, Finland, and Canada, will tend increasingly to use all their own timber output. In the past the tendency all over the world, and particularly in Britain, has been to grow trees for timber only and to use this land sparingly if at all for other purposes.

The first Scottish wood pulp mill has just come into production on a site near Fort William, but a chipboard factory, established at Inverness in 1963, has unfortunately been closed down. The demand for pulp wood and the increasing use of semi-synthetic timber materials should gradually remove much of the necessity for the production of clean timber by close planting, and there will be an increase in clear felling and replanting on short rotations. Needs for big timber can perhaps be met by high pruning of selected stems.

With the increase in importance of pulp mills there is also a trend towards siting fast-growing plantations on fertile sites, which may even be land of agricultural quality, near the mills, and to diversify the uses to which forests in remoter areas are devoted. This is in part an economic move, since the returns from forests on poor ground are small, and in part the result of an increasing demand by the public for recreational areas.

We can thus visualize the segregation of three types of forest: the pulp forests, in which total volume of wood produced per annum takes precedence over quality, and in which the life of the plantation is terminated at the point where annual increments begin to fall away from the maximum; forests in which saw timber is the primary product, and recreation, in the widest sense, a secondary use; and, finally, forests whose prime use is for sport, viewing wildlife and other recreational activities, and in which timber production takes second place. Such zoning of forests might go a long way in solving both the economic and the ecological problems that beset forestry today.

In Britain there are signs of such changes, and while the forest devoted primarily to wildlife exists only on Nature Reserves, a trial, being undertaken by the Forestry Commission at Grizedale, Westmorland, is worthy of mention. In Grizedale the Commission operate a scheme in which roe deer are used (a) for trophy hunting (b) for venison, which was sold locally in 1967 at 4s 6d per lb. (c) for skins and horns, which are used in the manufacture of tourist souvenirs during the winter months, and (d) as an attraction for visitors who are interested in observing wildlife in its natural habitat. Furthermore, ponds have been excavated in suitable places to encourage wildfowl. Given that these activities bring a cash return to the people who pay for them, which is realistic in relation to their true worth, the revenue from varied use of wildlife might well exceed that from trees. If so, some timber production can be sacrificed in the production of a more varied forest more attractive to wildlife.

The report of the Land Use Study Group (1966) suggests that marginal uplands may become the recreational grounds of the future. Ryle (1966), however, in reviewing this report, maintains that the snag lies in the costly provision of modern services (see p. 100). His view is that the uplands will remain the cockpit of agriculture and forestry, with tourism an important local but poor relation. This has not been the experience in the Lake District, now designated a National Park, and there is no good reason why it should always be so in the Scottish Highlands. The Cairngorms development (p. 100) suggests that tourism may well become the rich relation.

Fast growing exotics in even-aged stands will undoubtedly continue to form the basis of the Scottish forest industry, but certain measures which may become desirable on economic grounds would, at the same time, help to counteract a few of the undesirable features of such a regime. Fertilization of the hill forests throughout the rotation may become normal practice and the species that are grown may be altered to suit even the smallest variation in site factors. Natural regeneration may come to be utilized if possible in second and subsequent rotations, and the use of species mixtures may be extended if this leads to greater productivity per acre.

Some reorganization of the administrative structure of the Forestry Commission has just taken place but it appears that the recommendations of the 1963 Trend Report on Forestry Research are not to be implemented. These would have brought at least part of the Research Branch under the aegis of the newly formed Natural Environment Research Council. It is disturbing to find that all state forestry in Scotland will be run from a centre in southern England and that no provision has been made for the establishment of a separate research centre in Scotland. (A Forestry Research Station is now to be established at Edinburgh under the aegis of NERC.)

A period of reorganization would also have been opportune for reconsidering the need for purely protection afforestation on difficult and inhospitable sites, linked to possible recreational use as visualized above, and for an extension of the research programme to cover the problems associated with such work.

5. Sport and the Game Animals

The only sports which have materially affected land use in the Scottish uplands are deer stalking and grouse shooting. Until the late eighteenth century the hunting of wild birds and other animals was carried out principally for food and only incidentally as a sport. Following on the pacification of the Highlands, the next one hundred years saw the emergence of the two cults of grouse shooting and deer stalking and the allocation of land entirely to these pursuits sometimes at the expense of the newly emergent pastoralism.

Over the last few decades there has been some decline in the economic importance of grouse, partly as a result of the gradual falling off in the numbers of birds on many moors and partly because of social and economic changes. There has, however, been a revival in the past five years.

Red deer have gained great publicity, firstly as a result of post-war poaching, and secondly on account of their depredations on farm land, brought about by undershooting and their exclusion from wintering grounds by forest fences and hydroelectric schemes.

RED DEER

Red deer in Highland Scotland present one of the most intractable of the many problems involving wildlife and the land. Red deer are large and have a high potential for increase; they are a famous game animal; they are a favourite with tourists and naturalists; they are mobile and cross the contours quickly so that they exploit mountain vegetation efficiently; they are potential competitors with farm stock and can raid farm crops; they are an important part of Scotland's heritage of wildlife; they need low ground and shelter in winter and come into conflict not only with agriculture but also with hydroelectric schemes and forestry; they browse forest trees and sometimes strip bark.

Red deer are thus viewed in very different ways by the many and varied users of land. The problem is to integrate the uses of deer with other land use so that the deer may be safeguarded and at the same time may contribute to the economy of Highland Scotland. The difficulties which prevent solution of the problem are lack of ecological information, compartmentalized thinking about land use, and ingrained attitudes to red deer.

The owners of Highland sporting estates in the second half of the nineteenth century were rich. It was a time when fortunes were made in the industrial south and it became fashionable to own a deer forest.

Immense amounts of money were poured into the building of hunting lodges in remote places and in constructing roads, bridges, and tracks. The sport of deer stalking evolved an excellent code of hunting which persists today, but failed to develop a system of management based on the ecology (population dynamics, habitat relationships) of the quarry.

Trophy hunting was the obsession and the tendency was to take too many of the best heads. The effect seems to have been a deterioration in the size of the antlers and in body weight. Since female red deer have no antlers, the hind shooting was thought of as an unfortunate chore and was left to the resident stalkers after the owner or tenant had returned to the south. The hinds were wanted mainly for the larder so that those in best condition (with no calf at foot), the yeld hinds, were selected. The genetic effect of this practice is not known but its immediate effect was to leave poorer animals to carry through the winter the calf crop of the following year. While no studies of the possible resulting loss of calves have been made, the assumption is reasonable by analogy with domestic stock in which poor animals are removed since their chance of carrying an unborn young to full-term is small. Further, most losses of red deer calves seem to take place between conception and birth, perhaps in late winter when the deer are in poorest condition. Where too few hinds were shot each year the deer population increased and overstocking aggravated the poor condition of some herds.

Reaction to the situation produced by too heavy a selection of trophy stags was various. First, many estates began to weed out inferior animals, usually stags with obviously poor heads. Second, some estate owners imported large park stags from England and the Continent of Europe in an attempt to improve the Scottish stock. But, since Scottish deer were living in a poor and deteriorating environment, the effect was little more than an increase in the potential for many-pointed heads, a potential which was only realized when the deer were given individual attention. Third, some estate owners began to feed their deer in winter and some still do. Winter feeding as a part of normal management raises several questions, none of which has yet been answered in Scotland. Is it economic, that is, does the outlay give a good return in terms of more or better deer? What effect does winter feeding have on individual animals? Does it enable them to forage more widely or does it concentrate them unduly to the detriment of the habitat? What proportion of the herd avails itself of the food? The effects of winter feeding on deer are unlikely to be simple; they certainly need appraisal in the Scottish hill land environment.

However, even these attempts at improvement were often nullified by the fact that deer do not recognize unfenced boundaries. Estate boundaries today are still jealously guarded, and only rarely has there been progress towards the joint management of a shared stock and the development of a common shooting policy.

It is not known how far red deer have been adversely affected by the changes in vegetation brought about by hill sheep farming (p. 39) since they are versatile feeders and are browsers as well as grazers. The chief effect of the changes has been to widen the gap between the amount of summer and winter forage. Probably it is in this way that red deer have suffered, especially in areas where the stocking of sheep is heavy.

The loss of tree cover, mainly by felling, over much of the Highlands has also reduced the amount of shelter available to deer in winter. Plantation forests fenced against deer do little to improve the situation. Indeed, where fenced forests have been established on the traditional deer wintering grounds the animals have either had to remain on the inhospitable upper slopes or overflow on to agricultural land. Likewise, the flooding of valleys in hydroelectric schemes has driven red deer to poorer ground or to agricultural land where they damage winter crops (see plates 16 and 17).

In south-west Scotland, where forestry is pushing into red deer country and where fencing against deer is uneconomic, the Forestry Commission has been forced to face the problem that this raises. Increasing deer herds in the more rugged parts of this area have begun to strip bark from Lodgepole pine, here used mainly as a nurse for Sitka spruce. To the Commission's credit, it has begun with the premise that deer and forests can exist together, and it is trying to adjust management practice so that this will be possible. Three aspects are involved: a management plan for the deer herds; a planting scheme that leaves some wintering ground for the deer; and an investigation into the causes and prevention of bark stripping.

Increasing incursions of red deer on to farm land, and the inhumane slaughter of deer by organized poaching gangs, finally brought about the Deer (Scotland) Act of 1959. In this Act poaching was at last made illegal and heavy penalties were provided for infringements, close seasons were instituted, and the Red Deer Commission was set up. The Deer Commission's function is both advisory and executive. The staff deal with day-to-day problems produced by the marauding of red deer on agricultural land; they also advise landowners what their annual cull should be, where best to site forestry fences, and so on. The Commission has carried on a country-wide census and classification of red deer begun by Dr Fraser Darling for the Nature Conservancy, and can now suggest realistic culling rates.

68

The Nature Conservancy have a research programme on red deer, the results of which are passed to the Red Deer Commission in order to help them provide advice on deer forest management. Much of the work is located on the Island of Rum, where the herd of about 1,600 animals is wholly under the Conservancy's control. The Conservancy has tried to improve the herd by selectively shooting one-sixth of the adult stock annually and by adjusting the sex ratio to unity. The one-sixth cull has been sustained, winter losses reduced to a low level, and the quality of the animals improved. There has, however, been a complicating factor in the removal of 1,700 Blackface sheep just before the research on deer began. Rum offers unusual opportunities for experiment, and it would be wise to use the island for those aspects of deer research which cannot readily be carried out on the mainland. For example, it would be most useful to know how the production of red deer varies with population size in a given area, and what the long-term effect on vegetation is both with and without sheep.

On the mainland the Conservancy has studied the reproductive rate of red deer in order to assess how far the findings on Rum are relevant elsewhere. In fact, it seems that red deer in many parts of Scotland have a realised reproductive rate of twenty per cent per annum, which is the same as that on Rum. This means that the one-sixth cull may have a wider relevance, and the Deer Commission have provisionally adopted this level of cropping in their advice to landowners, many of whom crop at a very much lower rate.

There are also projects on red deer in progress at Aberdeen and Edinburgh Universities and at the Rowett Research Institute. In all, there is much interest in red deer and a great deal of research work is in progress.

But given that we have or will have the necessary knowledge for good management the question arises—management to what end? The present thinking on what to do with deer tends to be coloured by attitudes which came into being in the 1880s. Assuming that some revenue is to be made from the deer (and a sure way of preserving the species is to make it a sustained economic proposition) there are broadly three ways of using them: for trophy hunting; for stalking for its own sake; and for meat; although, of course, these uses are not mutually exclusive.

Estate owners must accept that the antlers of wild red deer in Scotland cannot equal those from the best European forests, and this is likely to remain so for a long time. Without considerable expenditure and individual attention antler development must remain a product of the natural environment, although some improvement is possible by eliminating beasts with poor heads from the breeding stock and by maintaining a proper age structure. Insistence on bigger and better sporting trophies brings the danger of perpetuating some of the practices that have led to the present red deer problem.

Scottish deer stalking is in a special category among blood sports. In contrast to hunting in many European forests stalking in the Scottish Highlands is truly a pitting of the hunter's skill against a wild animal in a wild habitat. If hunters are to be induced to come to Scotland it is the stalking as such that must be emphasized. Mar estate in upper Deeside has recently tried this out, initially with some misgiving, since German hunters, used to large trophy heads, were among the applicants. In fact, the project has been a success and the German visitors have been delighted at the sport in spite of the relatively poor trophies. An emphasis on the satisfactions of the stalking itself also opens up the possibility of commercializing the cull of hinds. Further, by placing hinds on the same hunting basis as stags, some of the jealousies between adjacent estates might be removed and the possibility of co-operation increased. Unfortunately hind shooting must be carried out between November and January, a season of inclement weather. Nevertheless, the possibility remains almost untried.

Since many red deer herds in Scotland seem to be selectively undershot the sex ratio is biassed to the extent of two or three hinds per stag. This ratio is better for venison production than for trophy hunting, which requires a 1 : 1 sex ratio in order to preserve a suitable age structure in the stags (Fol 1964). As noted on p. 69, both Rum and mainland herds examined are replacing themselves at a rate of twenty per cent per annum. The sex ratio on Rum is now 1 : 1, which means that one in six of the adult stock can be culled annually. If the same rate of calf survival is assumed in a herd with five hinds to every stag the increase per annum is thirty per cent; that is, one in three or four of the adult stock can be culled each year.

Table 1 (from Lockie 1965) shows calculations of the returns to be expected from a hypothetical population of 1,000 red deer managed in a variety of ways. The basic data and assumptions used are given as footnotes to the table. Clearly, the largest gross revenue is to be got from a combination of sport and meat production, where both hinds and stags are regarded as sporting quarry. Meat production at current prices gives the lowest return but, with a more realistic price of, say, 4s per lb (8s 9d per kg)—the retail price in Germany (Hunter 1965) is nearly 10s per lb (22s per kg)—the gross revenue exceeds that from hill sheep. The outlay in cropping deer for meat alone could probably be made a lot less than that incurred in breeding sheep on the same ground. However, one must be wary of too great an increase in the number of breeding females since these may have special nutritional

Table 1. Potential Gross Revenues from Red Deer and Hill Sheep per herd of 1,000

Nature of Use	Sex ratio	Charge	Revenue
A. Stag stalking		£50/stag	2,750
Stags & hinds for meat	1:1	2s/lb	2,076
			£4,826
B. Stag & hind stalking		£50/stag	2,750
	1:1	£25/hind and 2 y. olds	2,050
Stags & hinds for meat		2s/lb	2,076
			£6,876
C. Primarily meat production	1:5	2s/lb	£3,496
D. Hill sheep—meat, wool and sale of animals for breeding			£4,000

Notes

1. Price of venison is that in 1965: with market propaganda the price to the producer could be doubled. (See p. 64 for roe deer.)

2. Reproductive rates from Mitchell (1965), Cameron (1923), and Lockie and Mutch (unpublished). These range between 26 and 40 calves entering the two year class, per 100 hinds. We have taken 35 per cent as an average.

3. A negligible adult mortality is assumed.

4. Weights of animals, clean, are as follows: stag 168 lb; 1-2 years old 98 lb; adult hind 112 lb; 1-2 year old 84 lb; male calves 84 lb; female calves 70 lb (Cameron 1923).

5. Sex ratio in calves is 1:1.

6. Annual cull in A and B is one-sixth, in the following ratios 62 per cent adults, 16 per cent second year and 22 per cent calves (Fol 1964); annual cull in C is one-quarter in the following ratios: 68 per cent adults, 15 per cent second year, 17 per cent calves.

7. £50 (stag) and £25 (hind) are thought to be reasonable minimum charges for the sport and for the services of a stalker.

8. The gross revenue for hill sheep excludes a Government subsidy of about £1,000.

9. 1 lb = 0·45 kg.

10. Data for hill sheep from Duthie (1964 and 1967).

F

requirements which can only be met by highly selective feeding on plants rich in, amongst other things, nitrogen. In acid soils and cold climates nitrogen accessions are limited, so that it is easy to remove more than is returned over any period. Roberts (1959) has claimed that the deterioration of Welsh hill land has followed a change of policy from the grazing of wethers only to that of breeding ewes only, and Darling (1955) suggested partial replacement of ewes by wethers in the west Highlands for the same reason. However, we cannot begin to assess this problem in red deer yet, for we do not know the nutritional requirements of breeding hinds.

There are, at a conservative estimate, 150,000 red deer in Scotland, so that the total venison available for cropping annually is over 3,000,000 lb (1,360,800 kg). It is not known how much of this is harvested annually at the moment. Jenkins and Watson (1961) suggested 10 per cent, but the proportion is probably much greater than this today. Since this cannot all be dumped on the market over the stalking season, deep freeze installations would be required at key points throughout the Highlands, and co-operation between landowners would become even more necessary.

The calculations are based on a calf survival of 35 per 100 hinds one year and over (that is, about 45 per cent of hinds of breeding age). This means that up to 55 per cent of the calves conceived do not survive beyond their first year. Red deer hinds are attentive mothers and provide some milk for the calf right through the winter, even when pregnant. The chance of post natal calf survival is thus good until the end of winter, although some deaths may occur if the weather has been severe. Most of the 55 per cent loss thus probably occurs before birth. Presumably, abortion or reabsorption of the embryo is closely related to the bodily condition of the mother, which in turn is related to the quantity and quality of available feed.

Improved management should increase calf survival by giving the unborn calf a better start and by providing a better environment over the first winter. This involves manipulating both the deer population, as already explained, and also the vegetation on which they depend for food and cover. The management of red deer for different purposes in different parts of Scotland is in its infancy, and although the information required is becoming available experiments are now necessary to see how far, with a given environment, calf survival, adult mortality and adult body weight can be varied with different management.

There are a number of ways in which the habitat could be improved permanently (in contrast to the temporary improvement afforded by winter feeding). Some would be expensive and it is difficult, with present knowledge, to say what the economics of such improvements would be, since we do not know precisely how the deer would respond. A dramatic response by red deer to improved environment has been quoted by Lowe (1961). In 1870, seventeen calves were introduced from Invermark in Scotland to the virgin environment of South Island, New Zealand. The average weight of stags on Invermark at that time was 13 stones 1 lb (83 kg) and 14 pointers were rare. Fifteen to twenty years later the immigrant stags in New Zealand weighed over 30 stones (190·5 kg) and carried up to 20 points.

Methods of hill land improvement for farm stock by reseeding, fertilization, and fencing have already been discussed (p. 47). Not only is this expensive but also care in grazing management is required if the reclaimed land is not to deterio rate rapidly. It is doubtful if any of the existing schemes cater voluntarily for the needs of wintering deer, so that a special grazing regime would have to be devised if such joint management were contemplated. It is not known to what extent grazing of improved hill pastures by deer could be controlled.

The provision of trees and shrubs for shelter and understory browse would be a long-term possibility, but it would face immense problems in Highland Scotland. There is no tradition of conserving unplanted woodland and scrub, although something of the sort was practised by the people on a small scale prior to the coming of the Blackface and Cheviot sheep. The total acreage of all forest is small in relation to numbers of deer and domestic stock, and the planted forests remain vulnerable to certain types of deer damage, such as rubbing and bark stripping, after the leading shoots of the trees are out of reach.

Scattered throughout the Highlands are the small remnants of birch woods with willow, rowan, oak, hazel, and other species, usually on damp, north-facing slopes where fires do not reach. They provide some cover and browse but, with concentration of both deer and domestic stock on the ground, regeneration is usually absent, and the shrubs, too, are rapidly disappearing. Many of these woods have already vanished and the remainder are doomed unless small areas can be fenced to allow a new generation of trees to arise. Such an area was fenced against red deer, but not roe, on the Beinn Eighe Nature Reserve some ten years ago. Abundant regeneration of a few woody species such as rowan was obtained and the area is now a favourite haunt of the roe deer, which browse extensively on the saplings. It remains to be seen whether the roe will prevent any of the saplings reaching tree size or whether a sufficient number of these will get away and ensure the perpetuation of the woodland.

The problem of commercial forests is more difficult to solve in terms of dual use, since deer in numbers cannot be tolerated in young plantations and, even thirty years later, will strip bark from maturing trees. The reasons for bark-stripping are probably various, but the answer in most places may simply be shortage of adequate food. Understandably the Forestry Commission has refused to open such forests to red deer. They are, however, investigating bark-stripping in an attempt to discover its cause or causes. The work includes the provision of mineral licks in case the deer are seeking in bark, minerals in which they are deficient. In the North Conservancy of the Forestry Commission some deer are being let into plantations, in order to see how small numbers of deer behave towards trees in contrast to their extremely destructive behaviour after massive break-ins during hard weather. The problem is extremely important since, if deer must at all times be kept out of planted forests, the cost of repairing deer fences indefinitely will be high.

Mutch (1967) has suggested on grounds of efficient forestry that the units planted should be much larger than most are at present, thus greatly reducing fencing costs. Large units also have the advantage that the deer within them can be managed as part of the forest, and forest management modified in ways that may well reduce damage to trees. For example, wintering grounds along the edge of rivers can remain unplanted, and in a larger area there will probably be room for greater variation in the tree species used, with the possibility of avoiding those that deer prefer in areas where deer damage is likely.

Much of the poorer and high-lying hill land that will never produce commercial timber is nevertheless badly in need of tree cover. If amenity and protection forests could be utilized to some extent by deer and farm stock, the initial heavy cost of establishment would be offset by a slightly increased revenue. In addition, if the Government seriously believes that red deer should be managed and it accepts that red deer use some hill land better than domestic stock, then there is no reason in principle why subsidies should not be made available to initiate approved herd and habitat improvement schemes.

What kind of forest is needed that can give shelter and browse and, above all, can be opened to deer at an early age? Only a forest of dense thickets and open glades can even begin to meet the requirements. In this type of forest, the majority of established trees would be regarded as expendable, and utilized as animal fodder instead of being used as thinnings. A thicket of trees and shrubs which has been browsed back to a low cover would, if dense enough in places, provide protection for the odd tree to grow away to maturity (plate 18).

Such forests exist here and there in Scotland. For example, on the north side of Lochmore on Westminster Estate, Sutherland, the late Duke of Westminster planted an amenity forest of about 300 acres (120 ha) using a very wide range of conifers and hardwoods. All were

74

planted in thickets of varying size, sometimes so densely that neither man nor deer can push through. A small number of red and roe deer have found their way into the forest and are tolerated. Scots pine, Lodgepole pine and rowan are heavily browsed but only on knolls where they make poor growth anyway. The result is an extremely varied forest with heathery and grassy glades which are ideal for wintering deer.

The Nature Conservancy have a similar trial on the Beinn Eighe National Nature Reserve, Wester Ross. In an attempt to get tree cover quickly they have used Forestry Commission techniques of deep ploughing. Unfortunately they have also planted in rows, the resulting plantation being no different from any commercial forest—and just as vulnerable to deer. Here and there, however, as a trial they have planted thickets of whin and broom mainly to improve the site, but also as browse in anticipation of an entry by deer at some stage. If one can see beyond trees as a means to timber only, these tests are invaluable in pointing the way in which the Highland habitat may be improved for red deer and other animals.

Two centuries of misuse have changed the composition of the vegetation on Scottish hill land (p. 37). In all but the traditional grouse moors of the north-east, heather has tended to disappear and be replaced by *Nardus*, *Molinia*, and deer hair sedge. A standard method of habitat improvement is to ease the grazing pressure and allow desirable species to return. In this case we should wish to see more heather and, generally, a greater variety in hill vegetation. This may well require initially a considerable reduction in the stocks of red deer and domestic stock.

It has been emphasized on p. 42 that such a recovery of the vegetation is painfully slow and unsatisfactory under the soil and climatic conditions prevailing in the Scottish hills. Since it proceeds so slowly, we urgently need range methods for assessing the direction or trend of vegetational change under the influence of grazing animals. This might be done by concentrating attention on key forage species which respond to different intensities of grazing in characteristic ways. Linton (1918) has already detailed the value of many moorland plants to the hill sheep and has implied that variety is beneficial.

Over the past two centuries, although sheep have remained the primary use of the uplands as a whole, locally the swing from deer to sheep and back again has been abrupt. In one sense this could be described as a rotational use of hill land and it is unfortunate that forests have never played any part in these changes. However, one use at a time does not fully exploit the habitat except under really intensive land use. Recent official reports (*The Countryside in 1970*, 1965, Natural

Resources Symposium 1961, Advisory Panel on the Highlands and Islands 1964) all stress the need for multiple land use in order to obtain maximum sustained yields. Confining our attention to grazing animals, for the moment, the argument has repeatedly been advanced that in areas of Africa, where the annual rainfall is 30 ins (760 mm) or less, with a prolonged dry season, the cropping of game can give a better return for outlay with less damage to the habitat than the use of the land for pastoralism or subsistence agriculture. The ecological basis of the argument is that fifteen or twenty species of game animals all feed in different ways, so that all edible plant material is utilized. More than this, some species of game animal by their grazing prepare a suitable habitat for other species (Lamprey 1963, Fitzgerald 1960). While in practice this is probably an oversimplification, the general point holds that a variety of species exploits the habitat more fully than do few species and the native animals may be the more efficient converters of the vegetation in the long run. In the same way, it has been suggested that in arid Australia the native kangaroos are adapted to recurrent drought in a way that the introduced merino sheep is not and that they might have a place in outback pastoralism; all that is required is a better market for kangaroo meat and hides and further inroads on the wool market by synthetic fibres.

Transposing these ideas to Scotland it is evident that sheep, red deer, and cattle will together use the habitat more fully than do any of these alone, provided the difficulty of sufficient winter fodder can be overcome (but see the doubts expressed about reindeer introduction on p. 52). Cameron (1923) said this forty-three years ago and Darling (1955) described the ill-effects on hill land of a change in the sheep–cattle ratio (brought about by hill sheep subsidies and a boom in Harris tweed) from 15:1 in 1911 to 30 or 40:1 in 1946. Likewise, Hunter (1960) maintained that the trouble with the Highlands was not the presence of sheep so much as the absence of cattle.

There is a widespread belief in Scotland that deer dislike land soiled by sheep. But there are large areas of Scotland where deer and sheep intermingle in winter. It is true that deer seem to avoid by day areas where the stocking of sheep is very heavy, for example, the calcium-rich 'islands' in otherwise acid land. This may signify little more than that the sheep, which are close grazers, leave nothing for the deer to eat, or that deer descend to graze such pastures only at night when they are less readily seen. Research is needed into the feeding relationships of sheep and red deer, and into the circumstances of stocking density and habitat under which competition does or does not take place. Yet, thinking about the use of hill land remains largely compartmentalized.

76

We must, however, accept that some forms of land use can be incompatible (p. 104) and red deer management and tourism may well be one example. There is a tradition of unrestricted access to hill land in Scotland but, because in the past relatively few people could take advantage of this, conflict between landowner and public was slight. The Highlands, previously out of the reach of most ordinary people, are now easy of access, and the numbers moving to the open spaces at holiday times increase every year. There is also an increasing demand from the public for participation in sports and recreation previously enjoyed by the rich only.

The Nature Conservancy finds it necessary to restrict movement of the visiting public to the Nature Reserve on the Island of Rum during deer census work in April, calf marking in June, and during the annual cull of red deer between September and the end of December. It should be noted that this restriction applies also to staff members not engaged in the red deer study. This localized restriction is accepted by most people as a research necessity. But if red deer are to be managed properly throughout the Highlands, census, marking, and culling programmes will be widespread, and some conflict of interest may arise.

If the management of red deer remains in the hands of a few people the restriction of movement on hill land will not be tolerated by the new generation of emancipated country-goers. They may begin to tolerate restrictions if the sport of deer stalking becomes available to all (it must remain among the more expensive sports) or if meat production is for the national good. Alternatively, certain hill paths could be opened during the census marking and stalking seasons; but this is not possible everywhere without interfering with deer management. There is a serious potential conflict here which, if not resolved, could make red deer management difficult or impossible in many Highland forests.

The adequate management and full use of red deer may need a change of outlook in estate owners and the employment of some extra staff. The marketing of venison needs co-operative efforts, deep freeze centres and modern, attractive packaging. The deer habitat needs improvement. All this will cost a great deal, especially to begin with, and progress may be difficult over the initial stages. The suggested ways of using red deer are ecologically sound provided that the basic information is available for each area and provided that management follows the directives of research. But where there are several possibilities, each capable of sustained yield (implying no damage to the habitat), science cannot decide between them. At this point what people prefer and what is economic become the important considerations.

Suppose then that we can decide on several acceptable uses of red deer and we produce population and habitat management plans for each, having regard to the ecology and economics of the situation. Direct subsidy and tax relief could be given to those owners who agree to follow one or other plan, a small proportion of the revenue being ploughed back into research on deer management problems. Those who decline to co-operate may go their own way, but should be heavily taxed for the privilege of doing so.

Leopold (1933) maintained that in the long run the well-being of the land is best served by those who own it because they have a personal stake in the outcome. We cannot apply this dictum unchanged to the management of red deer in the Highlands, where capital from elsewhere often props up inefficient practices that lead to difficulties for other land users. Marginal land is too easily damaged irreparably (much of it has already suffered this fate) and the effects of wrong and inefficient practices are too far-reaching to permit personal whim alone to dictate land use.

ROE DEER

Roe deer appear to thrive in a variety of habitats from mature forest to the open hill. They like open woodland, young plantations, scrubland and the birch thickets that sometimes take over where a forest has been clear felled.

In hill land, roe are mainly a problem to foresters through the browsing of young saplings and fraying of older tree stems. Browsing is serious if the leading shoots of young conifers are pinched out, because this deforms the tree. Where natural regeneration is being attempted browsing can be devastating. Fraying is done by the bucks when marking and defending their does before and during the rut. The bark is rubbed up to two feet above the ground and the young tree dies if damage extends into the cambium on all sides. Springy saplings with wide internodes, such as those of Lodgepole and Scots pine, poplar, beech, rowan, and larch, are the favoured fraying stocks.

In some forest areas control is still too often a matter of shooting any roe deer on sight, sometimes with a shotgun. Roe deer drives are still common during which does and young animals are often the main victims and wounded and disabled animals are frequently left to die. Snaring of roe, which is banned on Forestry Commission ground, is still practised elsewhere. In fact, roe deer are widely treated as 'vermin', although this attitude is changing.

Attempts at rational management and control have been made in the main by the Forestry Commission. Ken McArthur is the author of roe deer management plans which have already achieved good results in reducing damage in the south of Scotland. These are based on a close knowledge of resident deer and of the changing seasonal behaviour of the species. By selective shooting, the social structure in the roe population is stabilized as far as possible and this keeps fraying damage to a minimum. Unselective shooting, on the other hand, may allow competitive young males to enter the area with a consequent increase in damage.

The Forestry Commission has shown that it is possible for deer and planted forests to coexist and, in Grisedale Forest in the north-west of England, has gone further by allowing the public to view roe deer from high seats and by allowing some roe stalking under close supervision. The venison of roe killed under the management plan is sold locally and to visiting tourists, and the antlers and hides form the raw materials for a small local industry. This is an excellent example of a subsidiary use of forest land.

Much is still unknown about roe deer. We have no quick census methods; we do not know what influences their browsing habits; and the reduction of browsing damage by modifying forestry practice has rarely been tried in Britain, although it has in USA on white-tailed deer (Verme 1965).

OTHER GAME

Red Grouse. The red grouse is more closely linked with its food plant, heather, than the red deer is with any part of its environment. As a direct consequence of this, existing grouse moors show a greater modification and specialization of the original ecosystem than do deer forests. In the original vegetation of the Highlands red deer may have been fairly abundant, but the red grouse must have been thin on the ground and confined to the dwarf heather mat between the tree line and the altitudinal heather limit, and to the boggy areas of thin or absent forest cover on the low ground. They may also have taken advantage of the larger temporary clearings, brought about by forest fires, while these were in the heather-dominated stage of the vegetation succession. Deforestation presented the red grouse with new and extensive heather-dominated habitats at low levels.

As management for game became widespread heather-dominated communities were deliberately burned to keep the heather young and vigorous as cover and food for grouse. As pointed out on page 38 the overwhelming dominance of heather from sea level to 3,000 ft (900 m) on the free-draining slopes of the eastern Highlands results from a fairly precise combination of edaphic and climatic factors allied to the particular land use history of the region. But burning for grouse was also extended to the west Highlands where the climate and slope drainage make it unsuitable even when care is taken to reduce the more harmful effects. The outcome in the west has been a reduction rather than an increase in the amount of heather. This, together with the induced soil and peat erosion and other deleterious changes in the habitat, has resulted in a general decline of game animals and other wildlife. Osgood Mackenzie (1949), writing of the Poolewe district of Wester Ross in the nineteenth century, tells of large bags of grouse (and other wildlife now scarce or absent) which continued until early in the present century and then declined spectacularly.

The eastern Highlands have not escaped the general deterioration, although heather remains abundant there. Dismay at the falling numbers of grouse on the traditional moors of Angus, Aberdeenshire, Moray and Banff prompted the Scottish Landowners Federation in 1957 to finance research into red grouse for a period of two years, after which the Nature Conservancy took over the project and established their Unit of Grouse and Moorland Ecology jointly with Aberdeen University. From the start Dr Jenkins (who was in charge of the unit) and his colleagues resisted pressure to apply the study to the direct boosting of grouse numbers, rightly maintaining that only a full ecological programme would serve the purpose. Their approach was fully vindicated and within five years they were able to produce hypotheses which satisfactorily explained the majority of the observations in grouse fluctuations.

Briefly, it was demonstrated that the shooting of grouse over butts never exploited annual production to the full. This was evident because the grouse made an adjustment to a still lower level of numbers after the shooting season. The surplus birds were ejected to areas, marginal for grouse, where their losses were higher than the losses sustained by the residents. The numbers of residents on all ground remained fairly stable throughout the winter, losses among them being made good from the ranks of the birds that had been moved on. Just before the breeding season there was a second adjustment, usually to a still lower level, and this formed the breeding stock for the ensuing year.

Clutch size, size of eggs, hatching date, chick weights, and hatching and rearing success all varied from year to year. All tended to be larger in years with early nesting leading to good breeding success, whereas all were smaller in years when nesting was late (Jenkins *et al* 1963, 1967). In years of good breeding the adults survived well through the winter before the breeding season and they weighed more in the shooting season in the August following breeding; in years of poor breeding they survived less well. This suggests that the survival of chicks was conditioned by events affecting the adults before the eggs were laid, and this was confirmed experimentally by taking eggs from the nests of wild grouse on different study areas and hatching and rearing them in captivity (Jenkins, Watson and Picozzi 1964).

Food is the factor most likely to affect the condition of the adults and the quality of their eggs. The quality of heather in April is influenced mainly by growth in the preceding summer and Dr Jenkins and his colleagues found a significant correlation between breeding success one year and the growth of heather in the previous year. They concluded that in most years breeding success depended on the condition of the territorial breeding adults just before the eggs were laid. Furthermore, fluctuation in spring numbers from one year to another were not due to adult mortality, but were related to variable breeding success in the previous summers. However, the relation of recruitment to subsequent breeding numbers was indirect. Territorial behaviour provided a buffer, since a proportion of the autumn population did not achieve territorial and therefore breeding status.

The Grouse Unit have more recently attacked also the problem of why different moors have different average densities of grouse. In general, the moors on good soil-forming rocks always had good breeding success and breeding numbers were stable. In contrast, moors on poor soil-forming rocks showed instability, with recruitment by breeding determining more directly the size of the subsequent breeding population (Miller *et al* 1966, Jenkins *et al* 1967). That is, territorial behaviour as a buffer functioned more strongly in 'good' as opposed to 'poor' habitats.

Clearly, grouse are extremely closely tied to heather, even if some of the effects of varying quantities and qualities of heather are buffered. Thus, if grouse decline in numbers over a long period, one might reasonably suspect a long-term decline in the quality or amount of heather, and this is one postulated effect of moor burning (p. 37).

Miller (1964) has reviewed the management of heather moors. From the game preservers' point of view the ideal size for a fire is about one acre (0·4 ha) since this, on a twelve year rotation, will give all the variations of young and old heather, for food and cover respectively, that a grouse needs on its 5-10 acres (2-4 ha) territory. Thus, the ideal on a 10,000 acre (4,047 ha) moor with a 10 to 12 year burning rotation would be 1,000 fires of one acre annually. Because of the statutory dates within which moor burning must take place, weather variations, and the availability of labour, this ideal cannot be approached on most moors today. Waddington (1958), writing on grouse moor management, states that he tries to burn 3,000 acres of his 50,000 acre grouse moor in 1,000 separate fires on a rotation of 16-18 years. The annual cost of this is £1,000. More usually, on the best managed moors, the fires vary in size from 5-10 acres near the keeper's house and 30-40 acres (12-16 ha) in more remote parts of the moor. In the west, where burning is practised mainly for sheep and deer, the fires are usually uncontrolled and many hundreds of acres may be burned at one time. Clearly, the size of fires must have a considerable effect on the numbers of territorial grouse that the moor will carry. It could therefore be argued that if, for any reason, there has been a tendency towards fewer, larger fires, this alone could explain the decline in numbers of grouse. However, the problem is more complex than that.

In order to maintain a consistently large stock of grouse the regeneration of heather after a fire must be rapid. Regeneration is affected by a number of factors among which the following can be important: the temperature of the fire; the age of the heather; soil type; local weather and climate; subsequent grazing by sheep, deer, rabbits and hares (pp. 37-44). Reference to the sections on moor burning and soil erosion will show that there are a number of factors which could have contributed to the decline in grouse numbers during this century. It is uncertain which are the more important and it may well turn out that all have played their part.

The economics of a 100,000 acre grouse moor have been given by Waddington, writing in 1958. Rates are high because the revenue from the sporting let is high; the annual costs of running the moor are around £14,000 and this about equals the rent. Cumming (1968) gives a more recent economic breakdown for his own 12,000 acre (4,800 ha) grouse moor. Expenditure is £2,900 p.a. and income £6,000. The return on capital is around three per cent. Jenkins and Watson (1961) have further outlined the fringe benefits associated with the sport, but an important question remains unanswered—does management for grouse give a sustained yield? Evidently it does not—hence the need for two grouse enquiries during this century. Thus, in comparing moorland used for grouse and for other purposes one must somehow fit a time scale into the comparison. For example, forestry might give a low but sustained return whereas grouse give a high annual revenue coupled with habitat deterioration. The cost of restoration of the habitat after 50-100 years, implicit in the difficulties of re-afforesting heather moors, must be debited to the revenue from grouse.

By reason of low soil fertility and inhospitable climate, forestry is the only alternative primary land use in most heather and grouse dominated districts today, although the extended period of heather dominance has brought about changes in the soil which make tree planting and forest establishment more difficult. It would seem that either expensive application of fertilizer to the moorland or a period under forest would be necessary to restore the grouse moors to their former productivity should this be desired. Above the planting limit, grouse with sheep and deer would seem to remain a valid land use combination although some continuation of moorland deterioration may have to be accepted if periodic burning remains the principal management.

In the long term grouse will probably continue to have their place in the economy of the Highland estates, but as a minor item in a wide range of enterprises and not as the hub around which the whole economy and land use pattern of thousands of acres revolves.

Ptarmigan. The arctic-alpine zone of the Scottish hills, where ptarmigan live, has been little affected by man. Even runaway fires from the low ground seldom reach far into this habitat. The ptarmigan is relatively lightly exploited although it lives at local densities as high as that of red grouse on the best moors. For example, Watson (1965), working in the Cairngorms, found local breeding densities of one pair to 5 acres (2 ha). More generally, the spring numbers fluctuated between 5 and 18 birds per 250 acres (100 ha).

Watson found that the numbers of ptarmigan stayed fairly constant from September until spring but decreased abruptly in March or April as soon as the winter flocks broke up and territorial defence began. The extent of the decrease varied from 18 to 47 per cent. Although predation by foxes and golden eagles was the only important adult mortality factor, it did not limit breeding numbers nor appreciably depress production. Neither was the level of the breeding population related to the current summer weather or to previous winter snow cover. Watson also found evidence of a ten year fluctuation. Breeding was good in years of increase and for the first years of peak numbers but was poor in later peak years and in years of decline. The sex ratio was unity in years of increase, but there were many more cocks and these were more aggressive in years of decline.

The food supply was not studied but, since it seems unlikely that a ten year fluctuation could be produced solely by climatic variation acting through food, some other interaction must be suspected. The longer amplitude of the cycle, compared with the four year cycle of voles in grassland, could be a reflection of the slower growth rate, and therefore recovery rate, of alpine vegetation in a harsh climate. This implies that the ptarmigan is interacting with its food supply, a hypothesis for which there is, as yet, no evidence.

There is little that one can do to manipulate the habitat for ptarmigan, but management could attempt to prevent the periodic peaks of numbers by heavy cropping as the population increases. In this way one might produce more stable populations and avoid the serious declines which follow abundance. If this proves impracticable, shooters can but try to crop a realistic proportion of the annual production with the knowledge that this is going to vary roughly 7-fold over a decade.

Mountain Hare. Mountain hares are widespread on the Southern Uplands, the Highlands, some Hebridean islands, Hoy in Orkney, and in Shetland. Mountains and high moorlands of grass or heather are the preferred terrain, mainly from 1,000 to 2,500 ft (300-750 m) altitude, but hares will range up to 4,000 ft (1,200 m).

In spite of the fact that large numbers of mountain hares are shot each season they have never been highly regarded as sporting animals in Scotland. Nor are they prized much as food, although many people will eat them. Large numbers of hares are fed to dogs or used as bait in traps. But fashions and tastes change and mountain hares may well become accepted more widely for food and sport as the number of hunters grows.

Man wages war on the mountain hare mainly because it competes with hill sheep for grass and heather. On moors and mountains hares are driven to guns early in the year but really big drives used to be more common and widespread. Less obviously, man affects the numbers of hares by changing the habitat through moor burning. On eastern grouse moors burning provides more young heather for hares as well as grouse so that the numbers of hares are often high and fluctuate widely, a fifteen to twenty-fold difference between the peaks and troughs being quite usual. While hares may be plentiful at about the same time as grouse are numerous, Hewson (1965) has shown that there is no marked synchrony of population fluctuation in the two species, but local differences in grouse populations could well confound this conclusion. Even where men kill a lot of hares the numbers fluctuate in a way which suggests that man's predation is not fully exploiting the hares' potential for increase.

In the west, and particularly the north-west, moor burning is more damaging to the habitat. This has almost certainly led to the present extreme scarcity of mountain hares in these parts. In fact, in Wester Ross, hares are now more numerous above than below the 2,500 ft (750 m) contour, which is a reversal of the usual order.

The more efficient cropping of mountain hares can at present only follow the lines suggested for ptarmigan. But even this will be difficult since the causes of short term fluctuations in the species remain obscure.

6. *Habitat and Wildlife Conservation*

To some extent an interest in Nature and the conservation of plant and animal life can be said to have grown out of the more atavistic interest in hunting. This chapter thus follows naturally upon a consideration of the game animals and their pursuit as a recreational rather than as a vital and necessary activity. Conservation is applied ecology, as indeed agriculture and forestry are, but in a still wider sense. If a conservationist were to be asked his basic philosophy he might well answer—the preservation and re-establishment of variety. Variety provides interest and it also gives stability to animal populations. As Elton (1960) has indicated, instability is most obvious in man-simplified habitats such as food crops and plantations, and in naturally simple habitats such as coastal tundra. By contrast, an old tangled hedge and bank rarely, if ever, suffers an outbreak of pests; it harbours not only the pest species but its enemies as well.

In Britain habitats are constantly being disrupted by the activities of man—by industrial development, roads, new towns, cultivation, tourist development, fires and grazing animals, and it remains to be seen how much is going to be left for wildlife. As Black (1966) has pointed out, the biggest conflicts are between development for cash gain and development for conservation purposes which may show no tangible return. In such disputes the conservation of nature rarely wins. The alternatives are either to change the criteria by which some land use problems are judged or attempt to put a cash value to the conservation of nature.

NATIONAL NATURE RESERVES AND THE NATURE CONSERVANCY

The Nature Conservancy was incorporated by Royal Charter in March 1949 following the acceptance in principle of a number of Command Reports on the conservation of British wildlife and its habitat. The basic list of Nature Reserves for Scotland is set out in the report of the Scottish Wild Life Conservation Committee (Cmd 7814). This list of suggested Reserves was not drawn up as a result of a comprehensive biological survey of the country (which was, in fact, another of the early recommendations and which was suggested as one of the functions of the Nature Conservancy), nor was there any suggestion that the areas put forward were the only, or even the best, surviving examples of each of the main ecosystems. The Committee did no more than bring together the combined experience and knowledge of the individual members and it is obvious that the greater part of the list was contributed by a small minority.

Some of the areas suggested as Reserves by the Wild Life Committee have not been declared by the Nature Conservancy, others have been declared with modified boundaries, and entirely new Reserves have been set up as a result of staff investigations and surveys. As the present list of declared and proposed Reserves stands there is little doubt that the country has missed its opportunity with a number of important habitat and community types, either because the formation of a national nature conservation organization came too late to save them or because the Nature Conservancy failed to take swift enough action immediately after its foundation; the forces of destruction always seem able to move more swiftly than the forces of conservation. Thus, the finest examples of oak and pine forest remaining in the country were sacrificed in two world wars or to the needs of the Forestry Commission for good quality plantable land. Oak forest of Reserve status along Loch Tay and in south-west Argyll was being felled in the early 1950s when the Nature Conservancy had still to acquire its first Scottish oak forest Reserve.

There is a perceptible difference in the background of conservation in Scotland, when compared with England and Wales, in spite of the unity of organization throughout the United Kingdom. Apart from one or two larger areas in the north of England and in Wales, Reserves south of the border are small, obviously greatly modified and sometimes quite artificial; they have often been set up to safeguard one species in particular or a group of rare species having a common habitat. In contrast the Scottish Nature Reserves are mostly large areas, more closely resembling the National Parks of other countries —and, indeed, the greater part of the Cairngorm Reserve is a National Park in all but name. They have at least some of the appearance of wildness, although this is almost entirely illusory, and the rare species are often more abundant in the surrounding country than in the Reserves themselves.

The main reasons for these differences are too obvious to call for comment, but one example can be used to illustrate the different approaches to conservation called for in the two regions. On chalk downland Reserves a constant battle is waged against scrub encroachment in order to safeguard species favoured by the man-made short grass sward, while in many Highland Reserves attempts are being made by sowing and planting to obtain tree and scrub growth for the amelioration of a stark environment which is again largely an artefact.

The Scottish Nature Reserves can be divided into two administrative categories: (*a*) those consisting of land purchased outright by the

86

Nature Conservancy; (*b*) those consisting of land that remains in private ownership (or State ownership under the control of another official body) and is managed by mutual agreement. The first arrangement is naturally the more satisfactory, the second too dependent upon the goodwill of the individual owners, their agents, or Government officials not always sympathetic to the idea of conservation. It should not be imagined that because a landowner enters into a Nature Reserve Agreement with the Conservancy he is looking only to the cause of conservation and understands all the considerations involved. Usually he has at least a vague and sport-centred interest in natural history but other motives, such as the desire to give his estate added protection against increasing numbers of holiday-makers or against State pressure to carry out afforestation, may be more important. Complications may also arise when such estates change hands and an entirely unsympathetic owner is obliged to inherit what is to him an irritating restriction upon his freedom of action.

The preparation of a management plan for conservation purposes over thousands of acres of hill land is difficult enough where complete control is possible, but where a compromise between conservation management and the continued running of an estate along conventional lines is involved the compromise is not really satisfactory to either party. The best that can be achieved is the maintenance of the *status quo* or the retardation of retrogressive changes in the hope that some future occasion may bring the estate onto the market and enable complete control to be obtained. Private action in conservation by enlightened landowners is, of course, valuable but cannot guarantee the same continuity of policy as can that of the State.

Nature Reserve agreements may be more satisfactory where the primary or sole reason for the establishment of the Reserve is the preservation of one or two threatened species whose future is relatively easy to ensure. For this reason these agreements are generally more satisfactory in England than in Scotland. Of course, if the preservation of the species requires the conservation of a large and complex habitat then the task is just as difficult as before.

Even in countries that have adopted a policy of nature conservation it is too often true that Parks and Reserves can only be established on land that is not required for other purposes, either because of its inherently low fertility, inaccessibility or climatic severity, or because it has been degraded by excessive exploitation to a point where it is no longer an attractive economic proposition. In Britain land for Nature Reserves can be acquired by the State only at a price agreed by the District Valuer and there is a tendency at the present time for land values to be inflated beyond an acceptable level. Even the poorest land in the Highlands may now command prices quite unrelated to its real value for agriculture, forestry, and sporting, and this tendency has sometimes been encouraged by agents through subdivision of derelict estates and advertisements designed to encourage the purchase of small areas from motives of romanticism.

Where land of any real economic value is acquired for conservation purposes anywhere in the world constant vigilance is required by the public to see that the conservation authority does not yield to the pressure of interests vested in grazing or timber concessions, hydro-electric development or real estate. Sometimes, as in the African Parks, it is possible to counter such pressure by the increasing monetary value of tourist interest in wild life.

The question of public access to Nature Reserves, as distinct from National Parks, can be difficult and relates to the general consideration of public recreation as a legitimate form of land use (pp. 98-102). Reserves may be open air laboratories, out-door museums, zoological gardens without bars, or National Parks according to the particular need or point of view. The ecologist values them as places where he may carry out long-term field experiments undisturbed and objects to unrestricted public access, knowing that it may lead to the partial or complete destruction of his work. The average National Park, which attempts to be both Nature Reserve and place of public recreation and instruction, demands rather a lot from the one area and may degenerate to the level of a large zoological garden or municipal park. Animals often become extremely tame and, while this can be a pleasant feature in many ways, the loss of extreme wariness is usually accompanied by the development of scavenging habits. Many people, too, would rather catch only a glimpse of the animals making for cover than see them begging for scraps by the roadside, and wildness may be essential for many ecological studies.

The Nature Conservancy conduct their Reserves on the principle that the public must be allowed maximum facilities consistent with the purpose for which each was established. In practice this may not be easy to arrange where the number of visitors is large and the Reserves small. There would often seem to be no alternative to a system of access by permit only or the zoning of larger Reserves according to the freedom of access to be allowed in each sector. The problem cannot be solved entirely by long-term education or by an application of mass psychology, although these must also be employed.

Another function of the Nature Conservancy is the delineation of any areas of geological or biological importance apart from those of Nature Reserve status. Existing legislation covering these so-called 'Sites of Special Scientific Interest' is unsatisfactory. Local authorities, having been advised by the Conservancy of the existence of an SSSI within their area under the Town and Country Planning Order of 1950, are obliged in their turn to notify the Conservancy of any projected change of land use involving the site. The main weakness of the legislation lies in the interpretation of the phrase 'change of land use'. As this is currently understood an area of native forest scheduled as an SSSI may be felled and replanted with exotics without notification having to be made, although a more intelligent appreciation of the situation by a local government officer may save the day. Any conflict of interests on those sites must be fought out at a Public Enquiry and, where financial considerations are great, the chances are strong that the decision will go against conservation. It is often difficult for the Nature Conservancy to present a case that will appeal to the public either in the original notification or at the subsequent enquiry.

It might then be asked what more the Nature Conservancy might be expected to do as the leading exponents of conservation theory and action in the United Kingdom. This can only be answered here in the most general way, but it does seem to us firstly, that some change in emphasis away from the more abstruse and academic lines of biological research and towards the more immediate practical problems of Reserve management is required; secondly, that the Conservancy could benefit by participation in a land use survey of the type suggested in Chapter 8; finally, and this could be the most telling project of all, a practical demonstration that ecological land use with conservation of natural habitat and wildlife is not incompatible with commercial agriculture, forestry and other activities. The last suggestion might possibly be attempted by the Conservancy out of its own resources of land and man power, for example on the island of Rum, or might form part of a joint project involving other Government organizations.

Conservation by other organizations. Sites of Special Scientific Interest, notified by the Nature Conservancy, may be adopted by local Authorities, such as County Councils, as Local Nature Reserves. This is an important contribution to the volume of nature conservation in England and Wales but has so far played a minor role in Scotland, where only about four Local Nature Reserves have been declared.

It is doubtful if the creation of National Forest Parks by the Forestry Commission out of some of their larger forests confers any extra protection upon the flora and wildlife of the area beyond what they would normally enjoy in an ordinary State Forest, and it may actually be deleterious through drawing public attention to the Forest. The Forestry Commission, like the Nature Conservancy, co-operates with neighbouring landowners in the destruction of foxes—purely for the sake of good relations, although it is contrary to their own interests since foxes prey upon mice and voles detrimental to regeneration and young tree growth. The Forestry Commission also, on their own account, attempt to control roe deer, black grouse and capercaillie, all of which do considerable damage to young plantations.

The National Trust for Scotland must be regarded as largely neutral where nature conservation is concerned. Within their properties, which now constitute a substantial acreage of the Scottish uplands, all forms of land use operating before the Trust's appearance continue, and special measures for the protection of native plants and animals are taken only in one or two areas of outstanding interest such as Ben Lawers and St Kilda, which are now leased to the Nature Conservancy as National Reserves. The recent purchase by the Trust of Torridon estate, which marches with the Beinn Eighe National Nature Reserve, may mark the beginning of a more active interest by them in the field of ecological land use.

At a 'Countryside Conference' in Inverness in April 1964 the National Trust suggested to the Secretary of State for Scotland that a standing working party should be set up to advise on questions of conservation and development.

A Scottish Wildlife Trust, set up in 1964, also establishes wildlife refuges. These supplement locally the nature reserves set up by the Nature Conservancy.

The Royal Society for the Protection of Birds is active in Scotland and is well known for its success with ospreys and snowy owls. It also administers some bird reserves, e.g. Handa Island in Sutherland.

MANAGEMENT OF VEGETATION

The expanding acreage of National Parks and Nature Reserves throughout the world is rendering it increasingly obvious that the science or art of managing natural vegetation for conservation purposes, as distinct from its long established management for pastoral, sporting or silvicultural reasons, has yet to be developed. Many reserves have been rendered ineffective, or their establishment has hastened the protected species to extinction, through failure to realize that setting aside a block of habitat and leaving it alone is not enough; paradoxical as it may seem, drastic and 'unnatural' action may have to be taken to keep a habitat effectively 'natural'. The habitat with its vegetation forms the stage and its scenery upon which the wildlife actors play their parts. We shall therefore look first of all at this aspect of conservation before considering the mammals and birds.

The manager of a National Park or other Reserve may be faced with one or all of a number of situations. First of all the species that he particularly wishes to encourage may be dependent upon a man-made habitat so that man's influence must be allowed to continue if the species are to remain. This is the situation with many of the rarer plants of chalk downland or mowing marsh or with the insects and birds of fens and coppiced oak–hazel woodland. Secondly he may find that an area has been so degraded by burning or logging or over-grazing that any action to improve the situation must be fundamental and far reaching. Recovery in some places may be surprisingly rapid but, at the other end of the scale, the retrogressive changes that have taken place may prove to be virtually irreversible even with the expenditure of large sums of money. We fear that this is the situation prevailing over large areas of the north-west Highland moorland. Finally, the problem may be merely one of increasing species diversity or of reducing over-abundant species of plants in a habitat that remains basically natural or semi-natural. This is the situation with most of the larger Scottish Nature Reserves. An over-abundant species which should be controlled in such areas is, for example, bracken.

The expedients open to the practising conservationist in vegetation management are the same as those used by foresters, soil conservationists, and pastoralists to manipulate the vegetation for their own particular purposes. These can be listed as follows:
(1) Improving or impeding drainage
(2) Irrigation
(3) Introducing or eliminating grazing and browsing through stocking or exclusion fencing
(4) Burning of dry vegetation
(5) Treatment of vegetation with total or selective herbicides
(6) Planting and seed sowing
(7) Cutting and grubbing out trees and shrubs
(8) Application of chemical fertilizers
(9) Small scale engineering works.
Using these methods he may find that he has to reconstitute a marsh, fen or bog that has been drained or burned and grazed. It may prove possible to restore a high water level, sometimes retaining it above the level in the surrounding country as in some English fens. Burning and grazing can be stopped but, in the case of retrogression of bogland, it may be found that a small quantity of phosphatic fertilizer is required to stimulate a new cycle of growth in the bog plants. This has been demonstrated on the acutely phosphorus-deficient terrain of the Beinn Eighe Nature Reserve.

Another common task is the redevelopment of grassland or heathland that has become overgrown with trees and tall shrubs following changes in some former biotic pressure. This situation often faces the pastoralist in other countries as a consequence of overgrazing of the more palatable grasses and other herbs. In this country trees and shrubs have been removed by hand in some of the Nature Reserves of southern England, and heather moor colonized by pine and birch is repeatedly restored to treeless moorland by controlled burning.

The rehabilitation and reconstruction of forests are routine tasks to the commercial forester and something has been said of this in an earlier chapter. Where the conservationist assumes responsibility for a logged and abandoned forest he may find no alternative to proceeding initially as the silviculturist does. Drainage may often be required, for example, since the natural drainage channels are frequently destroyed by heavy machinery. It may be difficult for him to decide how far to proceed with this knowing that many forests are naturally boggy and carry only stunted trees. In the same way the manager of a nature reserve faced with the task of restoring forest or scrub from heath, moor or bogland formerly under forest has to decide to what extent it is legitimate and practicable for him to employ the full range of treatments open to the forester in establishing commercial plantations. A great deal can often be done by simple seed sowing and fertilization methods as has been shown by the Nature Conservancy in the establishment of the common alder on wet moorland on the island of Rum and in the Beinn Eighe Reserve.

Finally, engineering techniques may be necessary to counter erosion where soil stability is required for the initiation of vegetation succession. The Nature Conservancy have hardly begun to develop this line in conservation although there is considerable scope available, for example, in the landslips of Rum. They have, however, carried out some studies on the stabilization of sand dunes at Braunton Burrows and of eroding peat in the north of England. A noteworthy Scottish example is to be found in the afforestation of the Culbin sands by the Forestry Commission, which was of course planned and executed as a commercial silvicultural proposition but which also shows just what can be done in the way of habitat restoration.

In some situations it may be sufficient to manipulate the habitat in order to produce the desired effects among the animal populations; in others it will be necessary to take direct action upon the animals themselves (see page 93). But even the design of an experimental programme for the elucidation of the factors involved requires an extensive knowledge of plant and animal ecology. Furthermore, results from one region cannot always be extrapolated to other areas although widely applicable guiding principles may be obtained from the first trial. Often one will be hampered by not knowing exactly what to aim for in attempts to repair mutilated ecosystems. It is certainly difficult to find examples of vegetation manipulation with the appropriate conservation orientation in this country.

In less developed countries the areas chosen for conservation will be relatively untouched and management will be reduced to a minimum. This will presumably be so in the new Kinabalu National Park in Sabah and in the older Taman Negara Park in Malaya. At the other extreme, devastated country may have to be rehabilitated at considerable expense if nothing better is available. In this case the action required will amount to a sort of ecological landscape gardening. In the long settled areas of Europe artificial habitats may have to be perpetuated since these have come to possess distinctive assemblages of species now in their turn threatened by technological man; the Broads of East Anglia are a case in point. The conservationists of the Netherlands have long since mastered the art of artificial habitat management.

Even a piece of completely untouched country may be difficult to maintain as a going concern if it is not large enough. The question of Reserve size and even siting is particularly important from the point of view of the larger territorial and migratory animals (as in the Serengeti National Park with the Ngorongoro Conservation Area). It may also be important in any effort to preserve representative areas of tropical primary forest where we are unable to define the minimal area of the plant association or enumerate all the species.

The management of an area primarily for habitat and wildlife conservation does not absolutely preclude the use of the area for other purposes, especially if these other uses have prior right of occupation. This theme will be developed in a later chapter. Thus, there may be limited timber exploitation, cropping of certain wild animals for sport or even commercial purposes, as distinct from cropping as part of the actual management, some recreational use, and even pockets of human occupation with concomittant cropping and the grazing of domestic animals. Each situation must be taken on its merits and a management plan drawn up to include an allocation of priorities.

CONSERVATION OF MAMMALS AND BIRDS

The conservation of nature in general and of animals in particular passes through three phases. First is a period of protection brought about by the swing away from past excesses which have made some species rare. The rarity may have been produced by exploitation for cash gain, by the destruction of the habitat, by wholesale killing of the animal as a competitor, or by 'luxury' destruction such as egg and skin collecting. This is a time of legislation to protect birds and other animals and the setting up of sanctuaries and nature reserves where the animals are inviolate.

The next stage comes when people begin to realize that nature is dynamic and that, in a man-modified countryside, wild animals may have to be managed. This may mean sometimes protecting, sometimes killing, or sometimes leaving alone. The realization of the need to manage implies an acceptance of the fact that the very success of protection can change the status of a rarity to that of a pest and that changing values and land use practices are often more important in determining the status of an animal than is legislation.

Finally, there is the period of multiple use, or the use of land simultaneously in as many ways as possible. This is the stage where nature conservation becomes accepted as a legitimate form of land use. While nature reserves continue to be refuges for wildlife and sites for ecological research they may well include tourism and sport. But nature conservation is also carried outside the nature reserves and sanctuaries; in true multiple use it becomes integrated with agriculture, forestry, tourism, sport and other uses of land (pp. 107-9). This is no easy task, for the basic facts which allow multiple use of land are not always known. However, multiple use implies variety, and variety favours the conservation of animals.

These phases in the development of conservation practice are, of course, not clearcut. They overlap, so that we may find imaginative schemes for multiple use co-existing with extreme protectionism. Highland Scotland is probably entering the third phase now.

The golden eagle illustrates the need to look beyond mere protection in attempting to conserve a species, to go outside nature reserves and strike a tolerable balance between land use and the pest potential of the bird. While existing land use may favour the species, changes may be most harmful.

Although specially protected under the Protection of Birds Act 1954, the golden eagle is often illegally killed in remote hill country. As their territory may be between 4,000 and 18,000 acres (1,619-7,285 ha) few nature reserves in Scotland can hold a pair of eagles (Watson 1957, Brown and Watson 1964, Lockie and Stephen 1959, Lockie 1964b). Thus, the future of the golden eagle lies largely outside nature reserves.

The dangers to this species stem from two complaints against it; first that it kills lambs and, second, that it kills grouse. It is a noteworthy fact that eagles in the eastern Highlands, where wild prey is plentiful, rarely eat lambs whereas in the west, where wild prey is scarce, they do so regularly. Indeed, there are few pairs of eagles in Wester Ross that have not at some time brought lambs to the eyrie. The inference is that lamb is not preferred food and this is supported by the fact that, in the west Highlands, the eagles at whose eyries lambs do not appear are found to have local access to abundant prey such as rabbit or mountain hare (for example, on some Hebridean islands).

The appearance of lambs in eyries is not necessarily a sign of lamb killing, as can be shown by examination of the lambs brought in. If the lamb was killed by an eagle it shows a large area of bruised blood under the skin; if not, it shows only the talon marks. If the eyes are out, a crow has been at the carcase before the eagle; if the ears are chopped off, then a fox is responsible. Proceeding in this way, Lockie (1964b) estimated that, of 22 lambs brought to an eyrie in Wester Ross in five years, seven were killed by the eagles. These eagles hunted over an area occupied by 1,000 breeding ewes, so that the loss inflicted on the farmer by the eagles in this instance was negligible.

The winter food of eagles comprises a great deal of sheep and deer carrion. Indeed, it can be argued that since suitable live, wild prey is so scarce (Brown and Watson 1964) eagles depend entirely upon carrion, which is there because of the poor management of sheep and deer in difficult country. Thus, the future of the golden eagle in the western Highlands is closely bound up with the future of sheep farming and red deer management. Withdraw the sheep or improve the management of deer and, other things being equal, eagles will become scarcer. Indeed, this may have already happened in certain areas of Sutherland and Ross-shire. There is, however, a further complication in that the chlorinated hydrocarbon insecticides used in modern sheep dips have been implicated in the poor breeding success of eagles in the west of Scotland in recent years (Lockie and Ratcliffe 1964, and unpublished). The more powerful insecticides, such as Dieldrin, have now been withdrawn from general use in Britain and the study is being continued as Dieldrin gradually disappears from the environment.

In the eastern Highlands, in contrast, golden eagles are more closely linked to grouse moor management. Jenkins *et al* (1964) have demonstrated for grouse the truth of Errington's contention that superfluous birds are the most vulnerable to predation. Since these are surplus to the carrying capacity of the heather habitat their destruction by predators or other agents does not affect the crop that the sportsmen will reap upon the Twelfth of August. While it may be unwise to apply these findings to all predator–prey relationships, the fact that they were worked out on a traditional grouse moor, where predators were not unduly scarce, demonstrates that the stupid and continuing war against avian predators serves no purpose in conserving the stocks of grouse.

Scotland is the showpiece of western Europe for its numbers of golden eagles as for other more obvious attractions. Is it not, therefore, worthwhile considering this species and its needs when planning land use?

The pine marten is a rare weasel which in the past suffered much from trapping and from the destruction of its habitat—mature forest. It is a good example of an animal which, given full protection in a nature reserve, nevertheless periodically becomes scarce. Its conservation can only be based on a sound knowledge of the animal and its relationship with its environment.

The small surviving population of marten in west Sutherland made an astonishing come-back between 1925 and 1946 when marten spread eastward to Caithness and south beyond the Great Glen. The impetus of this recolonization seems now to be spent. In the Beinn Eighe National Reserve the marten now show an apparent fivefold fluctuation in numbers over about seven years. After an abundance there is scarcity and this does not seem to be related to the fluctuations in numbers of the field vole, the main food. If we want moderate numbers of marten every year to show to visiting naturalists, management might consist in culling marten before they reach a population peak. Paradoxically, in order to have marten all the time one may have to kill a proportion at the correct time (Lockie 1961, 1964a).

No animal in Britain is more in need of conservation thinking than the fox. Outside fox hunting districts it is trapped, poisoned, snared, shot at and killed by terriers, for it undoubtedly takes lambs and game. Anyone might agree that this is reason enough for killing foxes at every opportunity, but the ecologist would want a little more information before passing judgment.

Lambs are the principal problem. The margin of safety between survival and death of sheep and lambs each spring in Highland Scotland is a narrow one and each year there are losses from starvation, accident and disease. On a 100 mile (161 km) transect in Wester Ross in early April 1965 we recorded fifteen dead sheep and five dead deer after an average winter. It is well known that the fox is a scavenger, an eater of lamb and mutton carrion, but the question to which there is still no answer is this: what proportion of these lambs is picked up dead and what killed by foxes? The ecologist would want to know what foxes normally eat, since it is obvious that they can live on lambs for only a small part of the year. In the Highlands they eat grouse, hares and rabbits, deer calves, lambs, deer and mutton carrion and large numbers of voles (Lockie 1963, Douglas 1965). Voles eat twice their weight in grass each day and so compete with sheep for the limited hill grazing.

Foxes do kill lambs and it is instructive to examine the circumstances in which lamb killing occurs. It happens in areas where wild prey is scarce and, in our experience and that of many hill shepherds, when the foxes are feeding cubs. It has been shown that if the cubs are destroyed lamb killing usually stops because the parents are no longer under pressure to provide food. This suggests a compromise control scheme for hill country in which lamb losses could be limited by destruction of the fox cubs while the adults were allowed to survive to prey on voles.

Many animals such as red grouse, roe deer, weasels and stoats are territorial and decide for themselves how many individuals shall live on a given area of ground. The surplus is squeezed out often to die in marginal (that is, barely suitable) habitats. Foxes are probably territorial and, if the adults are not persecuted, the numbers will level off; if all the resident foxes are killed, on the other hand, others will move in to take their place.

Small mammals, such as field voles, are hosts for the early stages of the tick which transmits 'louping ill', a virus disease that is a major veterinary problem on many hill sheep farms. Dr C. E. Gordon Smith and his colleagues have shown (Smith *et al* 1964) that these small mammals may be of particular importance as amplifiers of infection in years when their numbers are high. Firstly, when there are more voles, more ticks can feed and survive; secondly, a proportion of the tick larvae will become infected with the virus. Together, these will increase the risk of infection of sheep in subsequent years. A similar situation has been described in Czechoslovakia, where outbreaks of tick-borne encephalitis in human beings have followed 'mouse years' (Smith *et al* 1964).

Clearly, an agency that can flatten out the vole peaks will help to reduce the incidence of infective ticks. A strong and varied predator force of weasels, stoats, owls and foxes, given the chance, could be one such agency. The effect is even greater if the predators feed their young on nestling mice and voles, for these are the susceptible animals needed to amplify the infection.

Little is known about these relationships; we mention them to indicate that the bald statement that the fox is a pest begs a great many questions.

Many of the questions about foxes and lambs, and about the efficacy of control measures against foxes, could be answered if an area of hill land was set aside for a period of say five years with no attempt at fox control. Compensation could be paid for any loss of lambs during the period. It may seem incredible that we know so little about the fox and its effects on the countryside when 50,000 are killed annually in Britain; but the fox is difficult quarry for the ecologist.

7. Tourism

In recent years and particularly as a result of the 1965 conference 'The Countryside in 1970', recreation has become accepted in some quarters, if not in all, as a legitimate form of land use with a serious claim to consideration in land planning.

An increase in country recreation is a logical and inevitable result of affluence among city dwellers and also of population pressure. Britain has both affluence and population pressure. Study Group 9 (Countryside in 1970) has summarized the existing recreational demands on the countryside and, where known, the increase in demand between 1954 and 1964. The number of people skiing, riding, taking Outward Bound courses, camping, caravanning, and birdwatching has doubled or trebled in this time. The number of people who shoot or fish has increased by thirty-five and fifty per cent respectively, but facilities for these sports are less available and the demand cannot be met. These are all recreational activities which can be pursued on hill land.

But how should this new and expanding use of hill land be fitted into the scheme of things? Those who have a stake in the current uses of hill land insist that tourism must be integrated with the existing economy (Kemp 1965, Ryle 1966). This is an understandable view since, while the tourist is merely on holiday in the country, the countryman has his home and his livelihood there. Or again, the arguments are used: (1) that grouse shooting and stalking are enormous rural industries bringing a great deal of money and providing employment, and that this alone justifies their continuance as primary uses; (2) that sheep farming provides food for the country and that this alone justifies its continuance despite the fact that extensive hill sheep management has devastated much of the Highlands; (3) that forest plantations are necessarily an unchanging and primary use of land because the country needs timber, despite the fact that home grown supplies provide only five per cent of Britain's needs.

To use these arguments to preserve the *status quo* or to further sectional interests is just not good enough today. Scotland needs a basic land capability study of its hill ground in order to set the ecological limits on different kinds of use so that deterioration may be prevented on the one hand and full use achieved on the other. This is considered in greater detail later (pp. 103-12). Of course, economics, access, demand and facilities all must have their say in determining how the land will actually be used. Before this stage we need an ecological assessment; without it we cannot say how far practice falls short of the ideal.

In such an appraisal of land use, recreation should have a fair representation and not be treated as a poor relation to be squeezed in at the end if possible. The outcome of such a survey might be to indicate all variations from areas which could be given over primarily to tourism, to areas from which tourists should be excluded. The Tatra National Park in Slovakia has such a range of categories. In some areas forestry is the primary use and wildlife take second place; in other forested areas, wildlife conservation is the only use permitted and entry is by permit only.

Recreation, whatever its intensity, brings ecological, economic and psychological problems that planners would do well to heed. What do people want of an area they visit on holiday? How far does recreational use adversely affect the primary use of the area? Mutch (1967b) describes a survey he carried out in selected State forests in Britain in order to find out why people visited the forests at all, what they expected when they arrived, how much they were willing to spend to reach the forest, and the effect of tourist use on timber production.

The background to the survey was the major change in Forestry Commission policy published in the Forty-fourth Annual Report of the Forestry Commission in 1964. This was actively to provide the opportunity for public recreation in National Forests.

Broadly, there were two sorts of visitors, those who wanted peace and seclusion and those who wanted a picnic site and were not much interested in moving far from it. The first group wanted few facilities since these reduced the wildness of the area whereas the second group wanted car parks, lavatories, and open places for children to play in. In most of the production forests surveyed, the management changes required to accommodate tourism were surprisingly small. Apparently, satisfactory recreation can be provided in evergreen coniferous forests planted for timber production. The experience of foresters on the Continent of Europe suggests that fire is less of a hazard in forests heavily used for recreation than is generally supposed. In heavily used forests, car parks and open spaces which must be left unplanted constitute a loss to timber production, but a small one.

These findings will have a pronounced effect on the scale of development in each forest. Only certain forests justify complex and expensive facilities for tourists, but those that do should be thoroughly developed. At the other extreme, wilderness areas, which can only be penetrated with some physical effort, are a valid need for some people who have to be consciously catered for by deliberately keeping some wild land undeveloped. Mutch's survey showed that many of the worst fears of foresters, faced with a growing tourist pressure on forests, were unfounded.

The State Forest Service in Holland recognizes the need for adequate treatment of this new development. Each forest district has several senior staff, say, a production forester, an economist, a wildlife manager and an officer trained in recreational use of forests. All contribute to the running of the forests in the district, but which of the team is in charge depends on the primary use to which the forest is put. This seems a sensible approach to the multiple use of forests and one that the Forestry Commission in Britain might well adopt.

The problems produced by rapid development of tourism in hill country are most acute in the Cairngorm Mountains near Aviemore. Cairngorm itself has been sacrificed to tourism while Braeriach, a National Nature Reserve, remains undeveloped. This was a logical and reasonable development, since tourism in the form of hill walking and mountaineering had been developed for many years at Glen More Lodge on the lower slopes of the mountain. Moreover, since the summit plateau is around, 4,000 ft (1,200 m) snow lies late in spring and allows skiing for much of the winter.

In 1962, the Scottish Development Department invited Local Planning Authorities to safeguard beauty spots, to pinpoint development areas, and to stimulate the provision of facilities for visitors to enjoy the countryside. The Cairngorm area was such an area, and the Planning Authorities of Aberdeenshire, Banff, Inverness, Moray, Nairn, Perth and Kinross, together and by consultation with the many interested bodies, prepared the report, *The Cairngorm Area* (1967). While much development had already taken place before the report was begun, these authorities set out to describe the resources of the area and to suggest how they might be developed. The approach is perhaps unusual, though welcome, in taking note not only of development in the economic and material sense but also in considering the preservation of such intangibles as 'wilderness value', a disappearing commodity.

When Local Authorities have to encourage private investment in tourism in order to develop, development may not proceed evenly. The private investor wants a quick return so that profitable enterprises get attention while other development, necessary but less profitable, does not. Thus, skiers increased tenfold because chair lifts and tows were built. Accommodation was inadequate, but was then increased by 900 beds. Skiing slopes are now extremely crowded and the developers are casting their eyes farther into the hills for additional slopes. But this will reduce the wilderness value of the area since new roads must be driven in. What has not been decided is the point at which development stops in order to preserve the very commodity that attracts tourists. However, the Cairngorms report shows the needs and the priorities of development, and one would hope that further development will take place more evenly.

Perhaps the field in which the report is least satisfactory is in its lack of appreciation of the effect of people and machines on the stability of the countryside. The land around the White Lady complex of ski lifts and tows has been completely denuded of its vegetation over an area of about 800 acres. This has come about in several ways. First, bulldozers have been used to erect the lifts. Second, bulldozers are used each winter to push snow on to the ski runs when wind has blown them bare. Third, access roads for these bulldozers, like gigantic drains, have been driven straight up the hillside against all the rules of ploughing on steep slopes. Fourth, similar channels have been bulldozed up the ski tows in order to collect snow. Fifth, in order to pay its way the chair lift must be kept running in summer; many tourists go up in the lift and walk down. In places the vegetation is dominated by the moss *Rhacomitrium lanuginosum* and this is very easily destroyed by trampling.

The result is a series of large drains down very steep slopes devoid of vegetation. The 'drains' coalesce at the lower hut where the machinery is housed for the chair lift on the edge of the car park. Erosion has already begun under the chair lift and one of the pylons was slightly undermined in 1968. The real danger is from a quick thaw or a summer cloud burst. The ferocity of the floods, made worse by ill treatment of the catchment, can be seen at the foot of the hill below the car park. A similar down-pour now could carry the whole chairlift and car park into the bottom of the valley. The damage is so complete that only engineering works will save the day and this will be expensive. The authorities are conscious of the dangers but it is a pity that this result could not have been foreseen since ecologists, had they been consulted, could have advised on how to minimize the damage. Almost certainly this advice would have included a plea not to use the chair lift in summer. But this is presumably unacceptable economically.

The section of the report that deals with snow-fields describes the various kinds of snow, but one gets the impression that rather little information exists on the length of time that snow lies in different years and therefore the likelihood of good skiing in any year at an altitude which is, after all, just below the permanent snow line at this latitude. We would hope that meteorological studies are given a priority in order to put the assessment of snow potential on a firm basis.

Notwithstanding these remarks, the Cairngorms report is a model which should be followed by other councils before pressures arise and so that the councils can retain control of a changing situation. For example, one of the few remaining wild and remote areas of exceptional scenic beauty lies between Loch Maree and Dundonnel in Wester Ross. The area is privately owned, and was the subject recently of a dispute between the owner and the North of Scotland Hydroelectricity Board. The scheme was rejected, but had it gone through it would have meant roads driven into the centre of the area. One cannot consider this part of Wester Ross, however, without taking into account the coastline, the towns, the crofters, wildlife, and the tourists who use the area each summer.

This region, like so many others where pressures are mounting and development tends to proceed piecemeal and without much regard for amenity, needs a plan. Indeed, one has been produced recently by Glasgow School of Art Planning Department for the Scottish Tourist Board (1968). It is an interesting work, although we cannot agree with all the proposals. For example, this report suggests driving roads into the area behind Slioch in order to open it up for tourists. We believe its value lies in leaving it as it is. The important point is, however, that the report gives a basis for discussion which should lead to orderly development before it is too late.

To conclude, recreation is a legitimate form of land use and requires consideration in any appraisal of land capability. In this assessment, the traditional uses of hill land need not of necessity have priority in a rapidly changing situation. Given that the status of recreation *vis-à-vis* other uses is decided, the effects of people on soil, wildlife, vegetation and wilderness is extremely important for sustaining the industry. These effects can only be discovered by ecological research.

8. *Multi-Purpose Land Use and the Future*

The increasing interest in this country in ecological land use and conservation is shown by the recent introduction at four of our Universities of courses and research opportunities leading to diplomas and degrees in this inter-disciplinary field, The British Association for the Advancement of Science at its 1963 meeting in Aberdeen held a symposium on land use in the Scottish Highlands which was attended by the members of five sections: Geography, Economics, Botany, Forestry and Agriculture.

At this meeting Nicholson (1963) advanced the definition that sound land use is a system based on the ecological realities of the environment which produces something of direct economic, social or aesthetic value. From the ecological point of view the most appropriate use of any piece of land is that which most efficiently utilizes its particular edaphic, climatic and biological characteristics for man's needs and, at the same time, safeguards the first and last of these in perpetuity.

The concept of multiple land use may embrace either the accommodation of the maximum number of other possible uses along with the primary use, or it may involve local variation in the primary use to meet small scale variations in habitat factors. To some extent, then, a small country divided into many small parcels of land with different owners each pursuing different systems of management is practising multi-purpose use however single-minded in his utilization of the land each owner may be. It is difficult to say where one should draw the line, but we would suggest that it should be drawn short of the extensive areas of uninterrupted grouse moor, deer forest and conifer plantations typical of much of upland Scotland.

But how far are we justified in accepting as virtually axiomatic that multiple use of any piece of land is necessarily more desirable ecologically and perhaps economically than single purpose use or monoculture? Recent advances in plant pathology and expertise in crop husbandry, for example, have sustained a swing away from the concept of mixed farming held a mere two decades ago, and in some cases even the goal of maximum yield per acre has been shown to be economically less important than scale and specialization in the new factory farms. It cannot be denied that, at least in the short term and from the point of view of profits to the individual, this system works well in the more fertile districts, where high capitalization is possible, but it remains to be seen how far it will continue to oust diversified farming in less fertile areas and in a continually changing economic environment. Single purpose but far from intensive use of the marginal and sub-marginal lands of upland Scotland has lead to grouse disease, heather beetle outbreaks, sheep sick pastures, soil erosion, and a host of other problems: it is difficult to see how these can be rectified other than by diversification.

A limit is, however, set to the number of possible uses of a particular area by mutual incompatibility among them, and a limit to the number of contiguous or overlapping uses in an ecological mosaic can be set by economic, physical or even psychological considerations. Multi-purpose use can also lead administratively to the multiplication of a swarm of advisory and executive agencies, sometimes with un-co-ordinated policies and without effective overall control. This situation must be avoided.

The principal uses to which land in the Scottish uplands can be devoted may be set out as: hill sheep farming with or without cattle; crofting; grouse moor; deer forest; tourist recreation; forestry; habitat and wildlife reserves; water catchment for electricity generation and urban water supplies. Let us examine the extent to which these may be said to be compatible with one another.

Grouse and cattle, for example, are less compatible than grouse and sheep, principally because of the different food requirements of the two animals. Hill farming mixes reasonably well with deer forest and recreation but less well with forestry and wildlife conservation. Tourism is incompatible, at least seasonally, with grouse and deer, for obvious reasons, but there is no doubt that present antagonism could be mitigated by more widespread advertisement of shooting and stalking dates by the estates. Forestry is incompatible with sheep, cattle, grouse and deer, because trees are often damaged by browsing animals and they normally occupy all the sheltered wintering ground. Moor burning, too, makes foresters uneasy neighbours of sheep and grouse men. There is no reason, however, why forests, cattle and sheep should not be partly compatible once the trees have grown past their most vulnerable stage; a few private owners do practise a system of woodland grazing in semi-commercial forests. Wildlife conservation is incompatible with sheep and grouse, once again because of moor burning and also owing to the insistence of sheep farmers and grouse moor managers on predator destruction. Crofting fits well with hill farming, tourism and forestry, less well with deer forests, because of the problem of marauding deer, and with wildlife conservation, again because of certain predators and wild grazing animals. Agreement on red deer and fox control and the payment of compensation to the crofters, for example, for grazing damage by wild geese, is fairly easy to arrange, but there remains the problem of rarer mammal and bird predators. Once they have become established, hydroelectric installations are compatible with all other uses or can be made so with minor adjustments. Purity of water supplies from certain catchments requires some control over the recreational use of the same land.

Thus, grouse management and forestry emerge as the most difficult of these enterprises to integrate with the majority of other uses. The following measures would go far in obtaining the widest possible compatibility:

(*a*) Extreme care in moor burning. The areas burned to be kept as small as possible, preferably about one acre. Burning should not be done under the following circumstances: where bracken is becoming established; where heather is mixed with much *Molinia* and deer hair sedge (burning will not help to increase the heather but will eliminate it altogether); at altitudes where heather grows as a dwarf mat by exposure and is mixed with crowberry and azalea—a complete plant cover will not return in a man's lifetime; where steep slopes lead up to shrub-covered crags; and wherever the amount of bare peat and rock shows that erosion is already active (McVean 1959).

(*b*) Recognition by grouse managers and sheep farmers that the predator force is only a small factor in determining their success by comparison with others such as good management of heather.

(*c*) Opening of plantations to moderate grazing by deer and perhaps domestic animals once the trees have carried their leading shoots out of harm's way and provided the tree species are not susceptible to bark stripping. Areas where natural regeneration was being attempted could not be expected to sustain the same intensity of grazing.

(*d*) Provision of deer wintering ground in afforestation schemes and the provision of access to the low ground for deer as has been done in many places for sheep.

In summary, there are two main stumbling blocks in the development of multiple land use and an overall conservation policy in the uplands; these are the insistence on the part of the graziers and grouse moor owners on both moor burning and predator 'control' and the apparent inability of the Forestry Commission to carry out uneconomic or protection planting under the terms of its present remit. To these must now be added the widespread application of chlorinated hydrocarbons as insecticides and the strong probability that these are implicated in the increasingly observed lack of breeding success in many birds of prey (p. 95).

Large private estates with wide interests are in the best position for carrying out close integration of diverse enterprises and a few have already shown the way. Some steps towards integration have been taken by State organizations and there has been some give and take of land between the former Department of Agriculture for Scotland and the Forestry Commission, but the results to date are not impressive. The Nature Conservancy has co-operated with private landowners, but the absence of an economic factor in its existence has not placed it in a strong bargaining position with other State bodies which are, in any case, rather wary of too close an association with this collection of bird-watchers and cranks (as they too often wrongly see it).

The Conservancy-owned Isle of Rum could in time become an excellent example of the compatibility of forestry, agriculture, red deer management and overall wildlife conservation. An example of this kind, shown to be economically sound as well as desirable from the conservation point of view, will do more to further the cause of ecological management among other land users than any number of unsubstantiated claims.

There are also encouraging signs that those engaged in hill farm research are no longer insisting so dogmatically that present management of hill sheep causes no damage whatever to the upland ecosystems. In fact, the climate of opinion may now be favourable for some attempt to find a way in which moor burning can be reduced without damage to the hill sheep economy, where hill sheep happen to be the most appropriate land use. The Hill Farm Research Organization in its Third Report (1961–4) admits that the practice of burning *Molinia* has little to commend it and 'may be dismissed as a relatively harmless form of pyromania'. Grant and Hunter (1966) have recently suggested, from the results of heather clipping experiments, that the best form of heather management is to achieve a grazing intensity where about sixty per cent of the current season's shoot length is removed. In this way it is possible to keep heather physiologically young so that burning is unnecessary. In practice, however, the difficulties of controlling grazing so precisely over an area of hill land are great.

Closer integration of the Scottish Soil Survey with the vegetation work of the Nature Conservancy would be welcome. At the present moment the vegetation sections of the survey reports tend to appear as an afterthought, just as the soil data accompanying Conservancy vegetation publications are not systematic and lack the specialist touch. This need for liaison will apply increasingly as the Soil Survey covers more remote hill land.

If, as seems likely, the water yield of the Scottish upland catchments assumes greater importance in future, increasing attention will have to be paid to the soil and vegetation clothing these catchments, from this point of view. Already there has been some argument about the relative water consumption of grass and trees on English catchments, but this point seems a trivial one in comparison with the water wastage due to flash floods from deteriorated peat catchments in the north and west. True, improved catchment hydrology in the northern Highlands is not going to increase the water supply to Birmingham and Manchester, but the time may not be so far distant when water may have to be piped, more or less regardless of cost, from one end of Britain to the other. In the meantime the preparation of detailed management plans for vital catchments (beginning at the head-waters) should accompany the land capability survey advocated below (compare Gorrie 1958). The North of Scotland Hydroelectric Board has betrayed a lack of appreciation of this problem in the Highlands by not devoting some attention to erosion as a subject for research on the grounds that most of its water is derived from the higher-lying catchments. Apart from the fact that much of the trouble in catchment hydrology originates above the 2,000 ft (600 m) contour, the upper peat lands provide large quantities of suspended organic matter to the streams draining them, and the accumulation of this material in reservoirs must sooner or later have an effect comparable to that of normal inorganic siltation.

Land Capability Surveys

All over the world, farmers of marginal and sub-marginal land have tried to squeeze a living from soils unsuited to cropping and have usually ruined them in so doing. With a proper classification of the best and safest use to which land can be put, misuse can be avoided. Land capability surveys take into account the past use, climate, topography, soil type, slope and drainage, exposure, underlying rock, and the existing vegetation.

On this basis, the US Soil Conservation Service has drawn up an 8 point classification of land, summarized below in classes.

    I. Cultivation without special practices.
    II. Cultivation with simple contour practices.
    III. Cultivation with complex terraces, and so on.
    IV. Cultivation only with great care or limited use.
    V. Permanent pasture or woodland without special care
    VI. As class V, but requiring rotational grazing, restricted felling.
    VII. As class V, with severely limited grazing or highly
        selective felling.
    VIII. Wildlife only.

At first sight it seems that wildlife, for example, is relegated to the very poorest land. However, the scale refers only to the primary use of land. Any category higher on the scale than the one under consideration may be incorporated as a secondary or even a tertiary use. Thus, even on good farmland, some wildlife may be encouraged if only for sport. The classification of land capability given above may be applied equally to a single small farm or to a large land mass.

However, none of the existing scales, mostly based on the American system, can be used without modification in the Scottish uplands. An alternative scheme is given in table 2 and has been used in compiling figure 3.

All class VII land would not necessarily be set aside as Nature Reserves nor would existing Reserves automatically be classified as VII and be exempt from re-assessment. The only land that would be omitted from the survey in the first instance would be immature forestry plantations which would be difficult to assess and whose present use is obviously settled for some time. The most important task of the survey would be in distinguishing classes VI and VII from classes IV and V. Existing air photographic cover would help to some extent. Research is needed on the counter-erosion measures appropriate to classes VII and VIII.

A land capability classification is not final. There may be reassessment as new techniques in land reclamation and usage become available. Likewise, land use may be changed to meet a new need. For example, in some forests in the US recreation has supplanted forestry as the primary use. The obvious example in Scotland is the sacrifice of Cairngorm and the MacDhui plateau to tourism (skiing and hill walking) perhaps at the expense of wildlife (although this remains to be seen). But, if we decide to use class VII land for skiing and hill walking, the ecological restraints on the new use must be clearly understood. The increased use by people, the many human feet and the machines needed to build tourist facilities can do as much damage to vegetation as too many sheep and unwise burning; and we have excluded the last two from class VII land. Thus, if we upgrade tourist recreation to the primary use, we may do so only under very strict controls. No controls have been placed on either tourist or contractor use in the White Lady area of Cairngorm and a potentially very dangerous situation has developed (see page 101).

Thus, a land capability survey emphasizes the ecological constraints on the various uses of land. To ignore these constraints is to court disaster. Such a survey also designates which land is capable of what degree of improvement, having regard to presently known techniques.

The Scottish Peat and Land Development Association have sponsored a survey along these lines of the 130 square miles of moorland

Table 2. Land Capability Classification for the Scottish Highlands

Land capability & precautions in use	Primary uses	Secondary uses
I. Suitable for retention or reclamation as crop land. This would not necessarily imply that reclamation was economically feasible but only that it would be ecologically valid.	Agriculture	Recreation Wildlife Grazing
II. Suitable for improvement as grazing by cultivation and reseeding. Sub-class (*a*) mineral soils (*b*) peats.	Grazing	Recreation Wildlife
III. Suitable for improvement as grazing by methods other than cultivation. Sub-class (*a*) mineral soils (*b*) peats.	Grazing	Recreation Wildlife
IV. Suitable for retention as unimproved rough grazing in association with classes I-III. Position with respect to surrounding areas of the other classes would have to be taken into account. Careful moor burning permissible.	Grazing	Recreation Wildlife Watershed management
V. More suitable for commercial afforestation than grazing.	Commercial forestry	Recreation Wildlife Grazing Watershed management
VI. Suitable mainly for protection afforestation and wildlife. Moor burning not permissible.	Protection afforestation Wildlife	Recreation Grazing Watershed management
VII. Suitable only for wildlife. Moor burning not permissible.	Wildlife	Recreation Watershed management
VIII. Any areas requiring urgent counter-erosion works, including areas of severe peat hagging, badly gullied or sheet eroded slopes, landslips and river bank failures.	Erosion control Watershed management	

and farmland around the new town of Livingston, West Lothian. The object is to produce a programme of reclamation in the widest sense in order to upgrade the wet moorland to something more like a playground for the eventual 100,000 inhabitants of Livingston (SPALDA 1967).

A systematic land capability survey of the uplands has often been suggested and recommendations to this effect are embodied in several official documents such as Cmd 7976—Programme of Highland Development, Scottish Home Department, 1950. More recently a Land Use Commission, to function on an ecological basis, was suggested by Professor J. R. Mathews at the 1963 meeting of the British Association for the Advancement of Science in Aberdeen (Symposium on Land Use in Scotland).

It seemed at one stage as though the recently constituted Natural Environment Research Council would form a suitable parent body for such an organization. However, the omission of the Soil Surveys and any forestry component from NERC now make it seem less appropriate.

The existing soil survey of Scotland began, naturally, in the lowland farming areas and, if unaugmented, will be many years in covering all the more remote upland areas. Vegetation survey by the Nature Conservancy and Hill Farm Research Organization has not yet advanced beyond the definition of units with which to work and mapping has been confined to local exercises in the Isle of Rum and the Cairngorms (both unpublished).

We can thus envisage a suitable Land Capability Survey built up of units from an augmented Soil Survey, Nature Conservancy, HFRO and Forestry Commission (Research Branch) with appropriate administration. Further collaboration would be available from the Edinburgh University Department of Forestry and Natural Resources which is already carrying out exercises in land capability surveying. Problems revealed in the course of the survey could thus be tackled by the research staff of the appropriate organization as part of their own long-term research programmes. Such a composite survey team might be more acceptable to the land user than yet another State organization.

The next step after land classification is the zoning of land in order to prevent its misuse; this must be supported by adequate legislation. It may be thought that this is yet another restriction on the rights of individuals. The alternative is the destruction of marginal land, which it may be uneconomic and ecologically difficult to rehabilitate and which Nature unaided might take 1,000 years to repair.

Zoning of land according to its capability implies multiple use since even land suitable for crops has areas here and there which are waste for one reason or another. Such islets of waste ground must be actively managed to their potential (for example, for game animals, wildlife or erosion control) so that the total environment gives of its best.

The saddest feature of land capability surveys throughout the world is that their recommendations are seldom implemented. The volumes of reports are ranked on office shelves and colourful maps and charts decorate the rooms of the administration. The type of survey outlined above would be pointless without a complete change of Government attitude to the 'Highland problem' and all sub-marginal lands. There are signs that the Highlands and Islands Development Board subscribes at least partly to the old fallacy of local industrialization as a means of bringing the economy back to life. Without prior attention to the ecological health of primary land use, this and tourist development can only have what Fraser Darling (1955) described as 'macabre' results.

A SAMPLE CAPABILITY SURVEY

Vegetation and land capability maps of the Western Cairngorms have been included (figures 2 and 3) to illustrate the procedure outlined above. It may be useful to study this in conjunction with the maps and text of the *Cairngorm Area Report* (1967).

Figure 2 is based upon an unpublished vegetation map prepared between 1961 and 1963 by ground inspection and with the assistance of aerial photographs. Some simplification of the coloured original has been carried out. The base maps used were the One Inch series of the Ordnance Survey, and even at this scale distinct plant associations had to be grouped into complexes of closely related types to obtain areas of mapable size. The groupings now used are shown in the legend.

The land capability map (figure 3) has been prepared using the vegetation map as a guide and making use of additional information from topography and soils. It will be observed that there is a close relationship between the two maps but that the boundaries of vegetation types and land capability categories do not necessarily coincide. The effect of altitude is clearly discernible.

Land suitable for cropping is here confined to the alluvial flats of the River Spey and to certain pockets of glacial till derived from the schist mountains to the south and west. Granite till from the Cairngorm massif is more deeply podzolized and peat-capped and has seldom been brought into cultivation.

Between the crop land and the forest land lie areas where the local variations in soil and topography are such that classes II, III and IV

III

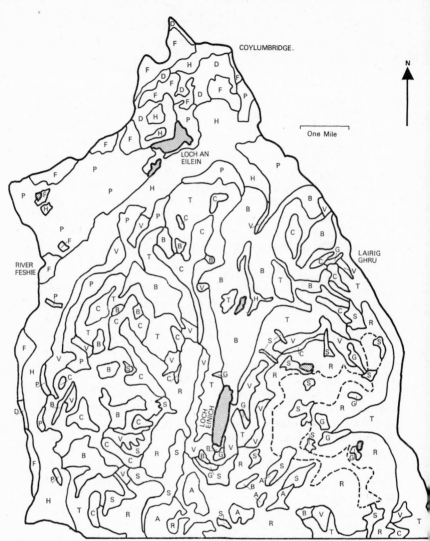

Figure 2. Vegetation map of the west Cairngorms.

A. Crowberry–cotton grass community of deep peat (27). B. Heather–
cotton grass community of deep peat (inc. comm. I on deep peat).
C. Dwarf heather community of exposed ridges (6). D. Natural birch,
alder, oak & planted decid. woodland. F. Crop & rotational grass
land. G. Natural grassland at high levels dominated by *Agrostis*,
Festuca & *Deschampsia caespitosa* (11, 18). H. Heather moor (4).
P. Natural pine wood & plantation. R. *Rhacomitrium*–mountain sedge

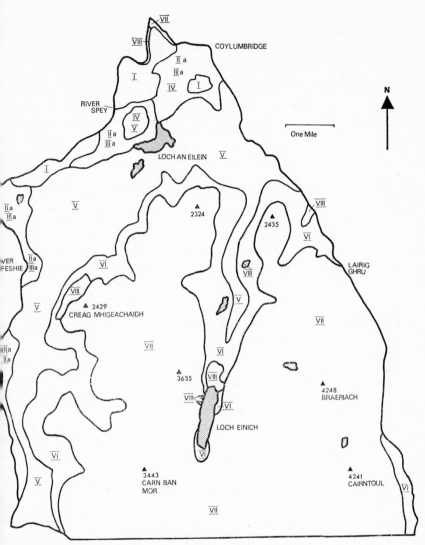

Figure 3. Land capability map of the west Cairngorms.

and *Rhacomitrium*–crowberry communities (10, 13). s. Late snow
complexes of *Nardus* with some *Vaccinium* at low levels (7, 20) &
Nardus with moss patches at high levels (20, 25). 1. Heather–deer hair
sedge community of shallow peat (28). v. Communities dominated by
Vaccinium and crowberry (7). Dotted line encloses tundra and bare
ground above 4,000 ft (22, 25). Numbers refer to vegetation types
(Chap. 1).

cannot be differentiated at this mapping scale. In the same way, small areas of alder swamp along the Spey and Druie should be designated VII but only one of these—at the confluence of the rivers—is large enough to be shown.

All the land above the potential forest limit has been classed as VII in view of the poverty of the soil, low nutritive value of the vegetation, climatic severity and shortness of the growing season. In less exposed regions of more fertile soils and more nutritive vegetation part of such terrain might be classed as IV. Small areas in this category do occur within the present boundaries (for example, Coire Odhar at the head of Loch Einich) but extent and accessibility must also be taken into account and they are disqualified on this score.

Land within the potential forest limit, some of it actually carrying pine forest at present, which is too steep and rocky, too high-lying and exposed or otherwise unlikely to be suitable for commercial timber production, has been classified under VI.

Class VIII land north of Loch Einich covers areas of deep peat hagging. The class VIII area below the crags of Creag Mhigeachaidh covers active gullying in stabilised scree and the small patches west of Loch Einich and at the north-west end of the Lairig Ghru cover similar cloudburst damage to the loose valley till. The strip of class VIII land along the River Spey west of Coylumbridge represents a line of river bank collapse in fertile soil.

The past use of the area does not agree with the zoning suggested. There has been much deforestation, heavy grazing and burning on class V, VI and VII land and the signs scar the middle slopes. As a result inherently poor land has been made still poorer.

List of Plant and Animal Names

Agrostis canina, A. stolonifera, A. tenuis, *Bent grasses*
Aira praecox, *Early hair grass*
Alchemilla alpina, *Alpine lady's mantle*
Alder, Alnus glutinosa
Alnus glutinosa, *Common or black alder*
Alpine lady's mantle, Alchemilla alpina
Anthoxanthum odoratum, *Sweet vernal grass*
Apodemus sylvaticus, *Field mouse, wood mouse*
Aquila chrysaetos, *Golden eagle*
Arctic hare, Lepus arcticus
Arctostaphylos uva-ursi, *Bear berry*
Aspen, Populus tremula
Bear berry, Arctostaphylos uva-ursi
Beech, Fagus sylvatica
Bell heather or heath, Erica cinerea, Erica tetralix
Bent grasses, Agrostis spp.
Betula alba, B. pubescens, *Birch*
Birch, Betula spp.
Bird Cherry, Prunus padus
Black grouse, Lyurus tetrix
Black locust, A leguminous tree, Robinia pseudo-acacia
Blaeberry, Vaccinium myrtillus, V. uliginosum
Bog myrtle, Myrica gale
Bracken, Pteridium aquilinum
Bramble, Rubus fruticosus
Calluna vulgaris, *Heather*
Capercaillie, Tetrao urogallus
Carex bigelowii, *Mountain sedge*
Carex spp., *Sedges*
Ceratodon purpureus, *A common moss*
Cladonia spp., *Common lichens including reindeer lichens*
Corsican pine, Pinus nigra var.
Corvus corone cornix, *Hooded crow*
Cotton grass, Eriophorum angustifolium, E. vaginatum
Crowberry, Empetrum nigrum, E. hermaphroditum
Deer hair sedge, Scirpus (Trichophorum) caespitosus
Deschampsia caespitosa, *Tufted hair grass*
Deschampsia flexuosa, *Wavy hair grass*

Dotterel, Charadrius morinellus
Early hair grass, Aira praecox
Empetrum hermaphroditum, E. nigrum, *Crowberry*
Erica cinerea, E. tetralix, *Bell heather, heath*
Eriophorum angustifolium, E. vaginatum, *Cotton grass*
Fagus sylvatica, *Beech*
Fescue grasses, Festuca spp.
Festuca ovina, F. vivipara, F. rubra, *Fescue grasses*
Field mouse, Apodemus sylvaticus
Field vole, Microtus agrestis
Fox, Vulpes vulpes
Golden eagle, Aquila chrysaetos
Heath, Erica spp.
Heath grass, Sieglingia decumbens
Heather, Calluna vulgaris
Heather beetle, Lochmaea suturalis
Holcus mollis, *Soft grass*
Hooded crow, Corvus corone cornix
Juncus articulatus, J. conglomeratus, J. effusus, *Common rushes*
Juncus squarrosus, *Heath rush*
Juncus trifidus, *Mountain rush*
Juniperus communis, *Common juniper*
Larix europea, *European larch*
Lemming, Lemmus spp., Dicrostonyx spp.
Lochmaea suturalis, *Heather beetle*
Lodgepole pine, Pinus contorta
Lyurus tetrix, *Black grouse*
Mat grass, Nardus stricta
Microtus agrestis, *Field vole*
Molinia caerulea, *Flying bent grass*
Mountain hare, Lepus timidus
Mountain sedge, Carex bigelowii
Myrica gale, *Bog myrtle*
Nardus stricta, *Mat grass*
Nettle, Urtica dioica
Oak, Quercus robur, Q. petraea
Osprey, Pandion haliaetus
Oxalis acetosella, *Wood sorrel*
Picea excelsa, *Norway spruce*
Picea sitchensis, *Sitka spruce*
Pine marten, Martes martes
Pinus contorta, *Lodgepole pine*
Pinus nigra, *Corsican pine*

Pinus silvestris, *Scots pine*
Poa pratensis, *Meadow grass*
Polytrichum spp., *Common mosses*
Poplar, Populus spp.
Populus tremula, *Aspen*
Prunus padus, *Bird cherry*
Ptarmigan, Lagopus mutus
Pteridium aquilinum, *Bracken*
Quercus petraea, Q. robur, *Oak*
Red deer, Cervus elaphus
Red grouse, Lagopus lagopus
Reindeer, Rangifer rangifer
Reindeer lichens, Group of branching Cladonia lichens
Rhacomitrium lanuginosum, *A common, grey, woolly moss*
Robinia pseudo-acacia, *Black locust*
Roe deer, Capreolus capreolus
Rowan, Sorbus aucuparia
Rubus fruticosus, *Bramble*
Salix herbacea, *Dwarf (Least) willow*
Salix spp., *Willows*
Scirpus (Trichophorum) caespitosus, *Deer hair sedge*
Scots pine, Pinus silvestris
Sedge, Carex spp.
Sheep tick, Ixodes ricinus
Sieglingia decumbens, *Heath grass*
Snowy owl, Nyctea scandiaca
Soft grass, Holcus mollis
Sorbus aucuparia, *Rowan*
Sphagnum spp., *Bog mosses*
Spruce, Picea spp.
Stoat, Mustela erminea
Sweet vernal grass, Anthoxanthum odoratum
Tetrao urogallus, *Capercaillie*
Tufted hair grass, Deschampsia caespitosa
Urtica dioica, *Nettle*
Vaccinium myrtillus, V. uliginosum, *Blaeberry*
Vaccinium vitis-idaea, *Cowberry*
Vulpes vulpes, *Fox*
Wavy hair grass, Deschampsia flexuosa
Weasel, Mustela nivalis
White-tailed deer, Odocoileus virginianus
Willow herb, Epilobium (Chamaenerion) angustifolium
Wood sorrel, Oxalis acetosella

Glossary

Acid rocks. Rocks containing a high percentage of silica and a low percentage of iron and magnesium minerals.

Acidophilous (plants and vegetation). Intolerant of waters and soils not markedly acid in reaction (pH greater than ca. 6·0).

Alluvial. Material deposited by running water.

Atlantic Period. A wet climatic phase beginning about 5,000 B C.

Basalt. A fine-grained igneous rock lacking quartz and rich in iron.

Basic rocks. Rocks containing a low percentage of silica and rich in iron and magnesium minerals.

Blanket Bog. The peat and its vegetation developed on flats and steep slopes alike and not dependent on the poor drainage of hollows.

Brown mosses. Reddish, brown and yellow, mostly prostrate mosses of the family *Hypnaceae* which inhabit damp ground of fair mineral status.

Carse land. Level, alluvial land along rivers.

Climax vegetation. The most complex and highly developed natural vegetation possible in any locality or region.

Colluvium. Rock debris collected against a slope as a result of falling and slipping from above.

Conglomerate. Rock consisting of rounded pebbles of all sizes in a matrix of sandstone.

Coppice. Growth from cut stumps of trees and large shrubs.

Dolomite. A rock consisting largely of magnesium carbonate.

Dominant (of plant species). The species which is physiognomically the most prominent in a community. It generally determines the micro-habitat in which the others grow.

Drift. see Till.

Ecology. Study of the relationships of living things to one another and to their physical environment.

Ecosystem. A particular assemblage of living things and the physical environment in which they live.

Edaphic. Relating to the soil.

Evapotranspiration. Water loss from any vegetated area as a result of combined evaporation from the soil and transpiration through the plants.

Feather mosses. Dry land mosses of the family *Hypnaceae*, mostly greenish, feathery and prostrate.

Fluvio-glacial. Material deposited by combined action of ice and running water.

Gabbro. A coarse-grained basic igneous rock.

Geological erosion. Soil and rock erosion which occurs in any climatic, biological and geomorphological context in the absence of interference by man.

Gley soil. Soil mottled bluish and reddish-brown due to occasional waterlogging and poor aeration.

Gneiss. Coarse-grained, metamorphic rock which is not laminated in structure.

Granulite. Coarse-grained, siliceous, metamorphic rock.

Greywacke. Type of sandstone with high proportion of felspar and other minerals in addition to quartz.

Grit (rock). Coarse sandstone.

Habitat. The location (with its attendant physical and biological characteristics) in which a living thing exists.

Hirsel. A one-shepherd unit on a hill farm.

Indicator species. Species of precise ecological requirements whose presence can be used as indicating the existence of a certain level of moisture, grazing, mineral nutrients, and so on.

Kelp. Large oar-shaped sea weeds found at or below low water mark.

Leaching. Removal of mineral substances by moving water.

Metamorphic rocks. Rocks altered from their original form by heat and pressure.

Moder-humus. Acid but biologically active humus.

Mor humus. Very acid, biologically inactive, part decomposed organic matter.

Mull humus. Slightly acid or neutral, highly active biologically.

Mycorrhiza. The structure formed by association of fungus with plant roots which is normally beneficial to both partners.

Mycostatic substance. An antibiotic limiting the growth of fungi.

Nadir river flow. Lowest volume of river flow reached in any given period.

Peridotite. Coarse-grained, ultra-basic, igneous rock.

Podzolization. Removal of iron, aluminium and plant nutrients from the surface soil by leaching.

Prothallus. Inconspicuous sexual stage of fern plants from which the familiar fern arises.

Rotational slipping. Downward slumping of rock or unconsolidated material, moving as one or more units, usually with backward tilting. That is, the movement is essentially rotational about a horizontal axis.

Sedentary soil. Soil developed *in situ* from the underlying bedrock.

Skeletal soil. Soil consisting largely of rock and undecomposed plant fragments.

Stool of shrub. Thickened stem base from which new shoots arise after burning, cutting, etc.

Succession (plant or vegetation). Process by which simple types of vegetation develop into those with a more complex structure. At the same time there is a convergence from wetter and drier than average soil conditions towards intermediate moisture contents and the development of a more fertile soil.

Till. The rock debris of glaciation varying from clay to gravel and boulder.

Ultra-basic rock. Rock lacking silica and consisting largely of iron, magnesium, and other heavy minerals.

Wether. Castrated male sheep.

Yeld. Not breeding (of sheep, deer hinds). Of red deer, strictly a mature hind with no calf at foot: that is, the question is left open whether the hind did not breed or whether she lost her calf early in pregnancy.

Bibliography

Advisory Panel on the Highlands and Islands. (1964) *Report.*
HMSO.

Albrecht, W. A. (1957) Soil fertility and biotic geography. *Geogr. Rev. 47*, 86-105.

Allen, S. E. (1964) Chemical aspects of heather burning. *J.appl. Ecol. 1*, 247-67.

Anderson, M. L. (1962) Forestry and land use policy in Scotland. Eighth British Commonwealth Forestry Conference. London.

Black, J. N. (1966) Sources of conflict in conservation administration. *Brit. Assoc. Ad. Sci.*, Annual meeting, Section D 1966.

Bower, M. M. (1962) The cause of erosion in blanket peat bogs. *Scot. Geogr. Mag. 78*, 33-43.

Boyd, J. Morton (1966) The changing image of the National Park. *New Scient. 30*, 254-6.

Braid, K. W. (1959) Bracken: A review of the literature. *Mim. Pub. No. 3/1959 Comm. Agr. Rev.*

Brown, T. (1963-4) The Red Deer Commission. *Scot. Agric. 43* (3) 131-5.

Brown, L. & Watson, A. (1964) The golden eagle in relation to its food supply. *Ibis 106*, 78-100.

Burnett, J. H., ed. (1964) *The Vegetation of Scotland.* Edinburgh.

Cairngorm Area (1967) *Report of the Technical Group on the Cairngorm Area of the Eastern Highlands of Scotland.* HMSO.

Cameron, A. G. (1923) *The Wild Red Deer of Scotland.* Edinburgh: Blackwood.

Chaffey, D. R. (1967) *The relative economics of forestry and agriculture on hill land in Scotland.* MSc Thesis. University of Edinburgh.

Cmd 7814 (1949) *Nature Reserves in Scotland.* Report of Scottish Wildlife Conservation Committee. HMSO.

Cmd 7976 (1950) *Programme of Highland Development.* Scottish Home Dept. HMSO.

Coppock, J. T. (1966) The recreational use of land and water in rural Britain. *Tydschr. voor econ. en Soc. Geog.* May–June, 81-96.

Cormack, E. & Gimingham, C. H. (1964) Litter production by *Calluna vulgaris* (L). Hull. *J. Ecol. 52*, 285-97.

Countryside in 1970, 2nd Conf. (1965) Countryside: Planning and Development in Scotland. *Report of Study group No. 9.* Royal Society of Arts and the Nature Conservancy.

Crofter's Commission Annual Reports (1956 onwards). HMSO.

Crompton, E. (1958) Hill soils and their production potential. *J.Brit.Grass.Soc. 13*, 229.

Cumming, W.G. (1968) The place of field sports in an estate plan. *Scottish Landowner 130*, 761-4.

Darling, F.F. (1937) *A herd of red deer.* Oxford.

Darling, F.F. (1955) *West Highland Survey: an essay in human ecology.* Oxford.

Darling, F.F. & Boyd, J.Morton (1964) *Natural History in the Highlands and Islands.* Collins New Naturalist. London.

Department of Agriculture and Fisheries for Scotland (1962) Scottish Peat. *Second Report of the Scottish Peat Committee.* HMSO.

Dickie, M.A.M. (1959) Rural development surveys in Scotland. *Forestry 32*, 53-64.

Dimbleby, G.W. (1962) The development of British heathlands and their soils. *Oxford Forestry Mem.* 23.

Douglas, M.J.W. (1965) Notes on the red fox near Braemar, Scotland. *J. Zool. 147*, 228-33.

Duthie, W.B. (1964) Report on financial results of 79 East of Scotland farms for 1962-3. *Bull. 77, Edin. School of Agric.*

Duthie, W.B. (1967) Financial results of East of Scotland Farms, 1965-6. *Bull. 87, Edin. School of Agric.*

Eggeling, W.J. (1964) Nature Conservation in Scotland. *Trans. Royal High. & Agric. Soc. 8*, 1-27.

Elton, C.S. (1927) *Animal Ecology.* London.

Elton, C.S. (1960) *The ecology of invasions by animals and plants.* London.

Fenton, E.Wylie (1935) The influence of sheep on the vegetation of hill grazings in Scotland. *J.Ecol. 25*, 424-30.

Fitzgerald, D.F.Vesey (1950) Grazing succession among East African animals. *J.Mammal. 41*, 161-72.

Fol, R. (1964) Aménagement du Grand Gibier. *Revue For.Fr. 6*, 451-73.

Geikie, A. (1887) *The Scenery of Scotland.* London.

Gibson, W.N. & Macarthur, K. (1965) Roe deer and methods of control in the forests of South Scotland. *Forestry 38*, 173-82.

Gorrie, R.M. (1958) Water resources and water needs in Scotland. *Nature 182*, 1193-5

Graham, E.H. (1944) *Natural Principles of Land Use*. New York.

Grant, S.A. & Hunter, R.F. (1966) The effects of frequency and season of clipping on the morphology, productivity and chemical composition of *Calluna vulgaris* (L) Hull. *New Phytol.* *65*, 125-33.

Green, F.H.W. (1963) Potential water deficit as a climatic discriminant in (ed. A.J.Rutter and F.W.Whitehead) *The Water Relations of Plants*. London.

Green, F.H.W. (1964) A map of annual average potential water deficit in the British Isles. *J.appl.Ecol.* *1*, 151-8.

Haldane, A.R.B. (1952) *The Drove Roads of Scotland*. Edinburgh.

Handley, W.R.C. (1954) Mull and Mor formation in relation to forest soils. *F.C.Bull. 23.* HMSO.

Handley, W.R.C. (1964) Mycorrhizal associations and *Calluna* heathland afforestation. *F.C.Bull. 36.* HMSO.

Heddle, R.G. & Ogg, W.G. (1936) Irrigation experiments on a Scottish hill pasture. *J.Ecol. 24*, 220-31.

Hewson, R. (1965) Population changes in the mountain hare *Lepus timidus* L. *J.Anim.Ecol. 34*, 587-600.

Highlands and Islands Development Board. *Annual Reports*. HMSO.

Hill Farm Research Organization. *Annual Reports*. Edinburgh.

Hunter, R.F (1962) Hill sheep and their pasture: a study of sheep grazing in S.E.Scotland. *J.Ecol. 50*, 651-80.

Hunter, R.F. (1964) Social behaviour and grazing management in hill sheep. *Advancement of Science 21* (90) 29-33.

Hunter, J.P.S. (1965) *Scottish Landowner 118*, 303-5.

Hutchinson, Sir Joseph (1966) Land and human populations. *New Scient. 31*, 465-9.

Jenkins, D. & Watson, A. (1961) Wildlife as a Natural Resource in Scotland. Scottish Council (Development and Industry), *Symp. on Nat.Res. in Scotland* pp. 187-93.

Jenkins, D., Watson, A. & Miller, G.R. (1963) Population studies on red grouse, *Lagopus lagopus scoticus* (Lath.) in North-east Scotland. *J.Anim.Ecol. 32*, 317-76.

Jenkins, D., Watson, A. & Miller, G.R. (1964) Predation and red grouse populations. *J.appl.Ecol. 1*, 183-95.

Jenkins, D., Watson, A. & Picozzi, N. (1964) Red grouse chick survival in captivity and in the wild. *Proc. 6th Congress Int.Union Game Biol.* Bournemouth, October 1963, pp. 63-70.

Jenkins, D., Watson, A. & Miller, G.R. (1967) Population fluctuations in the red grouse, *Lagopus lagopus scoticus*. *J. Anim. Ecol. 36*, 97-122.

Jones, E.W. (1945) The structure and reproduction of the virgin forests of the north temperate zone. *New Phytol. 44*, 130.

Kayll, A.J. & Gimingham, C.H. (1965) Vegetative regeneration of *Calluna vulgaris* after fire. *J. Ecol. 53*, 729-34.

Kemp, D. (1965) Highland Lairds and the Tourists. *The Scotsman* 27 February.

Lamprey, H.F. (1963) Ecological separation of the large mammal species in the Tarangire Game Reserve, Tanganyika. *E.A. Wildl. J. 1*, 63-92.

Land Use Study Group (Forestry, Agriculture and Multiple Use of Rural Land) (1966) *Report*, Dept. Educ. and Science. HMSO.

Leopold, A. (1933) *Game management*. New York.

Linton, A. (1918) *The grazing of hill pastures*. Selkirk, Scotland.

Lockie, J.D. (1961) The food of the pine marten, *Martes martes* in West Ross-shire, Scotland. *Proc. zool. Soc. Lond. 136*, 187-95.

Lockie, J.D. (1963) Eagles, foxes and their food supply in Wester Ross. *Scottish Agric. 42* (4) 186-9.

Lockie, J.D. (1964a) Distribution and fluctuations of the pine marten, *Martes martes* (L). in Scotland. *J. Anim. Ecol. 33*, 349-56.

Lockie, J.D. (1964b) The breeding density of the golden eagle and fox in relation to food supply in Wester Ross, Scotland. *Scot. Nat. 71*, 67-77.

Lockie, J.D. (1965) The use of red deer in Highland Scotland. *6th Intern. For. Congress*. Madrid (June 1965).

Lockie, J.D. and Ratcliffe, D.A. (1964) Insecticides and Scottish golden eagles. *Brit. Birds 57*, 89-102.

Lockie, J.D. and Stephen, D. (1959) Eagles, lambs and land management on Lewis. *J. Anim. Ecol. 28*, 43-50.

Lowe, V.P.W. (1961) A discussion of the history, present status and future conservation of red deer (*Cervus elaphus*) in Scotland. *Terre et Vie 1*, 9-40.

Mackenzie, O.H. (1949) *A Hundred Years in the Highlands*. London.

McNaughton, S.J. (1967) Relationships among functional properties of Californian Grassland. *Nature 216*, 168.

McVean, D.N. (1958) Island vegetation of some west Highland fresh water lochs. *Trans. Bot. Soc. Edin. 37* (3) 200-8.

McVean, D.N. (1959) Muir burning and conservation. *Scottish Agric. 39* (2) 79-82.

McVean, D.N. (1964) Ecology of Scots Pine in the Scottish Highlands. *J.Ecol. 51*, 671-86.

McVean, D.N. & Ratcliffe, D.A. (1962) *Plant Communities of the Scottish Highlands*. Nature Conservancy Monographs No. 1. HMSO.

Manley, G. (1952) *Climate and the British scene*. Collins New Naturalist, London.

Margalef, R. (1965) In (ed. C.R.Goldman) *Primary Productivity in Aquatic Environments*. California.

Miller, G.R. (1964) The management of heather moors in (ed. L.Dudley Stamp), *Land Use in the Scottish Highlands, Adv. of Science 21*, 163-9.

Miller, G.R., Jenkins, D. & Watson, A. (1966) Heather performance and red grouse populations. I. Visual estimates of heather. *J.appl.Ecol. 3*, 313-26.

Mitchell, B. (1965) Measuring the performance of stocks of wild red deer (*Cervus elaphus*) in the Scottish Highlands. *Proc. VIth Congress Int.Union Game Biol.* 163-6.

Mutch, W.E.S. (1966) Some effects of recreation demand on forest policy. Paper given at the 6th Int. Forestry Conf. Madrid. (June 1965).

Mutch, W.E.S. (1967a) The economics of wildlife management and forestry. *Suppl. to Forestry* pp. 98-102.

Mutch, W.E.S. (1967b) Public recreation in National Forests: a factual survey. HMSO.

National Trust for Scotland (1964) Countryside Conference, Inverness, April 1964.

Natural Resources in Scotland (1961) Symposium held at the Royal Society of Edinburgh, 1960. Scottish Council (Development and Industry).

Nature Conservancy. *Annual Reports*. HMSO.

Nicholson, I.A. (1964) The influence of management practices on the present day vegetational pattern and development trends. *Advancement of Science 21* (90) 18-23.

Nicholson, I.A. & Robertson, R.A. (1958) Some observations on the ecology of an upland grazing in north-east Scotland with special reference to *Callunetum*. *J.Ecol. 46*, 239-70.

North of Scotland Hydroelectric Board. *Annual Reports*. HMSO.

Parker, R.E. (1962) Factors limiting tree growth on peat soils. *Irish Forestry 19* (1) 60-81.

Phemister, J. (1948) *British Regional Geology, Scotland: The Northern Highlands.* HMSO.

Pigott, C.D. (1964) Nettles as indicators of soil conditions. *New Scient. 375*, 230-2.

Poore, M.E.D. & McVean, D.N. (1957) A new approach to Scottish mountain vegetation. *J.Ecol. 45*, 401-39.

Prebble, J. (1963) *The Highland Clearances.* London.

Radley, J. (1962) Peat erosion in the high moors of Derbyshire and west Yorkshire. *E. Midld. Geogr. 78* (1) 33-43.

Read, H.H. (1948) *British Regional Geology, Scotland: The Grampian Highlands.* HMSO (3rd. ed. revised by G.S. Johnstone, 1966).

Red Deer Commission Annual Reports. HMSO.

Rennie, P.J. (1953) Research into the physical and chemical properties of forest soils. *Rep.for.Res. 1952.* HMSO.

Rennie, P.J. (1957) The uptake of nutrients by timber forest and its importance to timber production in Britain. *Q.J.For. 51* (2) 101-5.

Rennie, P.J. (1962) Some long term effects of tree growth on productivity. *Emp.For.Rev. 41* (3) 209-31.

Richey, J.E. (1948) *British Regional Geology, Scotland: The Tertiary Volcanic Districts.* HMSO.

Ritchie, J. (1919) *Influence of Man on Animal Life in Scotland.* Cambridge.

Roberts, R.A. (1959) Ecology of human occupation and land use in Snowdonia. *J.Ecol. 47*, 317-23.

Robertson, R.A. & Davies, G.E. (1965) Quantities of plant nutrient in heather ecosystem. *J.appl.Ecol. 2*, 211-19.

Robinson, G.W. (1949) *Soils: Their Origin, Constitution and Classification.* London.

Rowett Research Institute. *Annual Reports.* Aberdeen.

Ryle, G.B. (1966) The use of our land. *Quart, J.For. 60*, 190-2.

Salaman, R.N. (1949) *The History and Social Significance of the Potato.* Cambridge.

Scottish Tourist Board (1968) *Planning Project No. 1: Gairloch, Wester Ross* (by Glasgow School of Art, Dept. of Planning). Edinburgh. pp. 136.

Smith, C.E.G., Varma, M.G.R. & McMahon, D. (1964) Isolation of louping ill virus from small mammals in Ayrshire, Scotland. *Nature 203*, 992-3.

Spence, D. N. (1960) Studies on the vegetation of Shetland, III. Scrub in Shetland and in South Uist, Outer Hebrides. *J. Ecol.* *48*, 73-95.

Speyside Drainage Report. Unpublished report by Dept. of Agriculture for Scotland on evidence gathered between 1952 and 1958.

Steven, H. M. & Carlisle, A. (1959) *The Native Pinewoods of Scotland*. Edinburgh.

Tomter, N. & Gorrie, R. M. (eds.) (1967) *Reclamation in the seventies*. Scottish Peat & Land Development Association.

Troup, R. S. (1952) *Sylvicultural Systems*. Oxford.

Turnock, David. (1966) Lochaber: West Highland growth point. *Scot. geogr. Mag. 82* (1) 17-28.

Udall, Stewart L. (1963) *The Quiet Crisis*. New York.

Verme, L. J. (1965) Swamp conifer deer yards in northern Michigan. *J. Forestry 63*, 523-9.

Waddington, R. (1958) *Grouse shooting and management*. London.

Wallace, R. (1917) *Heather and moor burning for grouse and sheep*. Edinburgh.

Watson, A. (1957) The breeding success of golden eagles in the North-east Highlands. *Scot. Nat. 69*, 153-69.

Watson, A. (1965) A population study of ptarmigan (*Lagopus mutus*) in Scotland. *J. Anim. Ecol. 34*, 135-72.

Watson, A. (1966) Hill birds of the Cairngorms. *Scot. Birds 4* (2), 179-203.

Watson, J. A. S. (1932) The rise and development of the sheep industry in the Highlands and North of Scotland. *Trans. Highl. & Agric. Soc. Scot.* Fifth Ser. vol. XLIV.

Whittaker, E. & Gimingham, C. H. (1962) The effects of fire on regeneration of *Calluna vulgaris* (L). Hull from seed. *J. Ecol. 50*, 815-22.

Index

Aberdeen University, *35*, *69*, *80*
Aberdeenshire, *9*, *80*, *100*
Achnasheen (West Ross-shire), *23*
Act of Union (1707), *6*
Advisory Panel on the Highlands
　and Islands, *76*
afforestation, *55-64*
Africa, *76*
alder, *55*, *57*, *61*, *92*
alpine lady's mantle, *19*, *20*
aluminium, *17*
Anderson, Professor M.L., *58*
Anglo-Saxons, *6*
Angus (County of), *80*
An Torc (Perthshire, Inverness-
　shire), *33*
Ardnamurchan (Argyll), *9*
Argyll, *7*, *86*
aspen, *57*
Australia, *7*, *76*
Aviemore, *35*, *100*

Banff (County of), *80*, *100*
basalt, *9*, *10*, *20*, *28*, *34*
bear berry, *42*
Beinn Eighe, *9*, *73*, *90*, *91*, *92*, *96*
Ben Lawers, *90*
Ben More (Assynt), *9*
Ben Nevis (weather records), *13*
bent–fescue grassland, *20*, *37*, *49*
Berwickshire, *16*
birch, *18*, *55*, *57*, *58*; *plates 2, 3,
　18*
bird cherry, *57*
Birmingham, *107*
Blackface sheep, *7*, *69*
black grouse, *see* grouse
Blacklaw Moss (Lanarkshire), *46*
black locust, *61*
blaeberry, *17-23*
blanket peat, *14*
boat building, *6*
bog bursts, *28*
bog myrtle, *21*
bracken, *18*, *40*, *44*, *91*
Braeriach (Aberdeenshire), *100*

Breadalbane, *20*
British Assoc. Adv. Sci: Land
　Use symposium (1963), *103*,
　110
broom, *75*
browsing, *73*, *75*, *91*
bunkers (erosion), *29*; *plate 12*

Cairngorm(s), *9*, *16*, *34*, *35*, *53*,
　83, *86*, *100*, *101*, *111*, *112*
Caithness, *8*, *9*, *96*
calcium, *12*, *76*
Cambrian (rocks), *9*
capercaillie, *90*
Carn Eilrig (Inverness-shire), *33*
carrion, *96*
carse land, *17*
cattle
　Highland, *6*, *52*
　hill, *52*, *59*, *76*, *102*
census (of red deer), *68*
chalk downland, *86*
chlorinated hydrocarbons, *105*
Clach Choutsaich (Inverness-
　shire), *32*
Clearances (Highland), *7*
Cnocan, *9*
Coire Cas (Cairngorm), *35*
coppice (oak), *55*
cotton grass, *9*, *18*, *25*, *31*, *38*, *45*
　bog, *22*
Countryside Conference (1964),
　90; (1970, Report), *98*
Creagan Doire Dhonaich (Inver-
　ness-shire), *33*
Creag Dhu (Inchriach, Inverness-
　shire), *32*
Cretaceous, *10*
Crofter's Act (1886), *7*
crowberry, *18*, *19*, *42*
Cuillins (Isle of Skye), *9*
Culbin Sands, *92*
Czechoslovakia, *97*

Dalradian rocks, *8-10*, *20*
Darling, Dr F. Fraser, *68*

Daviot (Inverness-shire), 33
deer, *see* red, roe
  hair sedge, *9, 18, 21, 23, 25, 38,
    40, 45, 105*
  (Scotland) Act, *68*
Department of Agriculture for
  Scotland (former), 106
diorite, *9*
dolomite, *9*
drainage, *28, 92*
Drumochter Pass, *27*
Dulnan, *16*
Duntulm (Isle of Skye), *34*
Durness (Sutherland), *9*

Edinburgh University, *69, 110*
Eire, *47*
Elphin, *9*
encephalitis (tick-borne), *97*
engineering (erosion), *92*
erosion, *16, 24-35*
evapotranspiration, *13-14, 30*

fencing, *47, 48, 59, 74*
fescue grass, *17, 19, 20*
field vole, *90*
Fionchra (Isle of Rum), *34*
floods, *16*
flying bent grass, *18, 20, 22, 38,
    40, 45*
Fochabers (Moray), *8*
Foinaven (Sutherland), *9*
Forest Lodge (Perthshire), *33*
Forestry Commission, *58, 64, 68,
    74, 78, 79, 86, 89, 92, 99,
    106, 110*
fox
  red, *83, 90, 95-7*
  arctic, *1*

gabbro, *9*
Galloway, *9, 14*
Germany, *70*
glacial till, *9, 34*
Glen Carron, *34*
Glen Docharty, *27*
Glen Tilt, *33*
Glenmore, *52, 100*
gneiss, *7*
golden eagle, *83, 94*
granite, *9, 28*

granulite, *8*
greywacke, *10*
Grisedale (Westmorland), *64, 79*
grouse
  black, *90*
  red, *7, 19, 41, 79-83, 104-5*
grouse moors, management of,
    81, 82
gully erosion, *27-8*

hag (peat), *25, 31, 32*
hare, mountain, *84*
  arctic, *1*
Hebrides, *95*
heath, *25*
  rush, *20, 40*
heather, *18, 38*
  moor, *19, 23, 32, 61*
  beetle, *40*
Highlands and Islands Develop-
    ment Board, *111*
Hill Farm Research Organization,
    46, 53-4, 106, 110
Holland, *99*
Hoy (Isle of), *84*
humus
  raw, *40, 42, 45, 47, 61*
  mild, *40, 47*
hydroelectric schemes, *17*

Inchnadamph (Sutherland), *34*
Inchriach (Inverness-shire), *33*
insecticides, *105*
Invermark, *73*
iron smelting, *6*
irrigation, *49, 91*

Jenkins, Dr David, *80*
juniper, *32, 40, 57, 58; plate 17*

kangaroo, *76*
kelp, *7*
Kinabalu National Park, *93*
Kincraig (Inverness-shire), *17*
Kingairloch, *9*
Kingussie (Inverness-shire), *33*
Kinross-shire, *100*
Kishorn (Ross and Cromarty), *9*

Lairig Ghru, *112*
lambs, *51, 94-6*

Lanarkshire, *46*
land capability, *2, 107-12*
landslips, *28-9, 112*
Land Use Commission (proposed),
    110
larch, *59, 61*
leaching, *4, 9, 11*
lemming, *1*
Lewisian gneiss, *7, 9*
Liassic, *10*
lichens, *21*
limestone, *8, 10, 11, 34*
Livingstone (West Lothian), *110*
Local Nature Reserves, *89*
Lochaber, *16*
Loch Einich, *112*
Loch Etive, *9*
Loch Laggan, *28*
Loch Maree, *102*
Loch Ness, *8*
Loch Tay, *86*
Lomond Hills, *28*
louping ill, *97*

MacArthur, Ken, *78*
machair, *29-30*
Macaulay Institute, *46*
Malaya, *93*
Manchester, *107*
Mar Estate, *70*
marten, *see* pine marten
mat grass, *18, 20, 21, 40*
meadow grass, *20*
mica-schist, *8, 20*
Moine rocks, *8, 10*
moor burning, *37-44, 59, 81-2,
    84, 105*
Moray (County of), *80, 100*
Morven, *8*
moss, *18, 19*
    heath, *18, 21-2*
mountain hare, *84*
mountain rush, *21*
mountain sedge, *21*
mudstone, *9, 10*
Mull (Isle of), *8, 10*
multiple use, *94, 102-11*

nadir river flows, *17*
National Forest Parks, *89*
National Nature Reserves, *34,
    85-90*

National Parks, *86, 93*
National Trust for Scotland, *90*
Natural Environment Research
    Council, *110*
Natural Resources Symposium
    (1961), *76*
Nature Conservancy, *68, 69, 77,
    85-90, 106, 110*
Neolithic period, *6*
Nethy Bridge (Inverness-shire), *29*
nettle, *40*
Newtonmore (Inverness-shire),
    33
New Zealand, *73*
Ngorongoro Conservation Area,
    93
nitrogen
    fertilization, *61*
    fixation, *61*
Northern Ireland, *62*
North of Scotland Hydro-electric
    Board, *102, 107*

oak, *18, 55, 57, 86*
Oban, *8*
Old Red Sandstone, *8*
Ordovician, *10*
osprey, *90*
owl (snowy), *1, 90*
Oykell Bridge (Sutherland), *59*

peridotite, *9*
Perthshire, *7, 100*
phosphorus, *12, 40, 45, 48, 49,
    60, 61, 91*
pine
    Corsican, *61*
    lodgepole, *61, 68*
    Scots, *18, 55-8, 60, 68, 75;
    plates 1, 17*
pine marten, *96*
podzol, *10, 11*
Poolewe, *80*
potassium, *61*
potato, *7*
predation, *95-7*
Protection of Birds Act (1954),
    94
protein synthesis, *2*
protein production, *2-5*
ptarmigan, *83*

quartzite, *8, 9*

Raasay, *10*
rabbit, *95*
ranching (cattle), *52*
Rannoch Moor, *9*
recreation, *98-102*
red deer, *7, 19, 21, 65-78*
  food and feeding, *67*
Red Deer Commission, *68, 69*
red grouse, *see* grouse
regeneration
  of bog, *91*
  of forest, *56-7*
reindeer, *52*
  Council, *53*
  food of, *53*
Rhacomitrium moss, *19, 21, 101*
ring barking, *55*
River Nethy, *29*
River Spey, *17, 111-12*
roe deer, *64, 78-9, 90*
Romans, *6*
Ross-shire, *22, 80, 84, 94, 95*
rowan, *57*
Rowett Research Institute, *69*
Royal Society for the Protection
  of Birds, *90*
Roy Bridge, *28*
Rum (Isle of), *8, 9, 34, 69, 70,
  77, 89, 92, 106*
Ruthven, *17*

Sabah, *93*
salmon, *16*
Scottish Landowners' Federation,
  80
Scottish Peat and Land Develop-
  ment Association, *108-9*
Scottish Plant Breeding Station,
  49
Scottish Soil Survey, *106*
Scottish Wildlife Conservation
  Committee Report, *85*
Scottish Wildlife Trust, *90*
screes, *26-7, 33*
Secretary of State for Scotland,
  90
Serengeti National Park, *93*
sex ratio, *70, 83*
shale, *10*

sheep, *19, 94-5*
  Blackface, *7, 49-52, 69*
  Cheviot, *7, 49-52*
  Merino, *50, 76*
sheep tick, *97*
shell sand, *30*
Shetland, *84*
Silurian, *10*
'Sites of Special Scientific
  Interest', *88*
skeletal soil, *11*
skiing, *100-1*
Skye (Isle of), *8, 9, 10, 16, 34*
slate, *8*
Slioch (Ross-shire), *102*
Slochd Mor (Inverness-shire).
  32, 43
Small Isles, *8, 10*
snaring (of roe deer), *78*
soil improvement, *61*
sphagnum moss, *18, 31, 56*
sphagnum bog, *23*
Sperrin Mountains (Northern
  Ireland), *29*
sport, *66-84, 93, 104-5*
spruce
  Norway, *59*
  Sitka, *59-65, 68*
  aphid, *62-3*
St Kilda (Isle of), *90*
stoat, *97*
Storr Rocks (Isle of Skye), *34*
Strathspey, *17, 111-12*
Sutherland, *7, 16, 22, 59, 74, 95*
syenite, *9*

Taman Negara National Park
  (Malaya), *93*
Tatra National Park (Slovakia),
  99
Torridon (Ross-shire), *90*
Torridonian sandstone, *8, 9*
tourism, *64, 77, 94, 98-102, 104*
Trend Report, *64*
trout, *16*
tundra, *85*
Turriff, *8*

ultra-basic rock, *9*
United States of America, *7*
u s Soil Conservation Service, *107*

vegetation, management of, *90-3*
venison, *64, 79*
Vikings, *6*
vole (field), *1, 83, 96, 97*

wavy hair grass, *20, 22*
weasel, *97*

Westminster Estate, *74*
whin, *75*
White Lady Sheiling (Cairngorm)
    35, 101, 108
white tail deer, *79*
wilderness, *99-102*
willow, *22, 57*
wood pulp, *63*

Captions to Plates

Plate 1. Typical dense native Scots pine forest, Rothiemurchus, Inverness-shire. Note the dominance of *Vaccinium myrtilus* and *V. vitis-idaea*. Several isolated plants of heather can be seen in the centre of the photograph.

Plate 2. Typical sheep-grazed west Highland birch wood near Kinloch-ewe, Ross-shire. Note the seed parent tree on left with pole stage progeny on right and uncolonized space between. The field layer consists of closely grazed *Agrostis–Festuca* turf with much moss.

Plate 3. Ungrazed birch–rowan wood on a small island in the Fionn Loch, Ross-shire. The tree stems are from coppice shoots. Compare the luxuriant growth of woodrush, ferns, herbs and grasses with the woodland floor in plate 2.

Plate 4. Sheep-grazed ash wood on limestone pavement near Tornapress, Ross-shire. Moss is dominant both on the rounded limestone outcrops and in the smooth *Agrostis–Festuca* turf between.

Plate 5. Typical heather-dominated hillside in the central Highlands. Note the uncovering of bedrock and natural scree as a result of burning and the patches of light-coloured erosion associated with sheep tracks (centre and top left). The lighter coloured vegetation in the gullies (centre and bottom right) is dominated by *Vaccinium myrtillus* as a result of the winter accumulation of snow in such sites.

Plate 6. End point of sheet erosion of shallow peat at 1,000 feet on the Cambrian quartzite of w. Ross-shire. Relict patches of peat remain (centre). The vegetation of the eroded surface consists of sparse and mineral-deficient heather, bell heather, and deer hair sedge, with mosses and lichens.

Plate 7. Slochd Mor, Inverness-shire. Destruction of pine and hardwood forest and grazing in the past led to the development of good bent–fescue turf on the brown soil, and juniper scrub and heather moor on the surrounding slopes. Today, under a regime of all-year grazing and burning, scree formation is proceeding rapidly on the heather slopes, the grass turf is broken and few junipers remain (Erosion site, p. 32).

Plate 8. Active gullying of a steep grassy slope in Glen Tilt, Perthshire, caused by sheep grazing and trampling across unstable colluvium (Erosion site, p. 33).

Plate 9. Nearing the end point of deep peat erosion in west Ross-shire. Some recolonization of the stone pavement is taking place.

Plate 10. Gully erosion of fluvio-glacial debris capped by shallow peat in the south-west Highlands as a result of burning and sheep grazing.

Plate 11. Contrasting areas on one hillside in Glen Carron, Ross-shire. The burned and grazed area on the right shows sheet erosion of the upper slopes with gullying below. The lower part has been fenced and planted but, without control of grazing above the fence, the gullies are liable to extend upwards and threaten the afforestation below (Achnashellach erosion site, p. 34).

Plate 12. A small patch of felled woodland has been heavily grazed by sheep. Sheet erosion and the formation of bunkers in the steep slopes are well advanced. The exposure of the tree roots provides some measure of the soil already lost (Newtonmore–Kingussie erosion site, p. 33).

Plate 13. Erosion of machair at Opinan, near Gairloch, Ross-shire. The rich sward is heavily grazed by sheep throughout the year. This, together with trampling, has broken the surface, allowing wind to complete the destruction of this extremely valuable resource.

Plate 14. Erosion caused by bulldozers, skiing, and human feet in the area of the White Lady chair lifts and ski tows, Cairngorm Mountains, Inverness-shire (Erosion site, p. 34).

Plate 15. Bracken spreading into a heather-dominated area near Garve, Ross-shire, after burning. The fire has also burned the thin peat layer thus exposing boulders that were previously covered.

Plate 16. Red deer stag on low ground in winter in the south Cairngorm Mountains. The pine forest is scanty and draughty and there is no regeneration. The ground vegetation is grazed short and hand feeding is practised. Losses are heavy in bad winters.

Plate 17. Good wintering ground for deer on the north side of the Cairngorms. The key to the management of the area, which is under snow for three or four months each winter, lies in adjusting the deer and sheep populations to the availability of browse species, juniper, birch, and heather.

Plate 18. A birch thicket naturally regenerated and under heavy pressure from cattle and sheep near Aviemore. Even with this intensity of browsing, trees in the centre of the thicket get away to perpetuate the birch wood.

Plate 1 Dense native Scots pine forest.

Plate 2 Typical sheep-grazed west Highland birch wood.

Plate 3 Ungrazed birch-rowan wood.

Plate 4 Sheep-grazed ash wood on limestone pavement
near Tornapress, Ross-shire.

Plate 5 Typical heather-dominated hillside in the central Highlands, showing erosion.

Plate 6 Sheet erosion of shallow peat at 1,000 feet on quartzite.

Plate 7 Scree formation, destruction of juniper and breaking of *Agrostis-Festuca* turf by grazing and burning.

Plate 8 Active gullying in Glen Tilt by grazing and trampling.

Plate 9 End point of deep peat erosion.

Plate 10 Gully erosion in the south-west Highlands as a result of grazing and burning.

Plate 11 Sheet erosion and gullying contrasted with intact afforested land.

Plate 12 Sheet erosion and bunkers on land previously forested and now heavily grazed.

Plate 13 Wind erosion of machair near Opinan, Ross-shire.

Plate 14 Erosion caused by tourism in the north Cairngorms.

Plate 15 Bracken spreading into heather after a burn.

Plate 16 Red deer stag on low ground in winter.

Plate 17 Good wintering ground in the Cairngorms.

Plate 18 Birch thicket, naturally regenerated and under heavy browsing pressure.